DATE			

THE BLACK RURAL LANDOWNER– ENDANGERED SPECIES

Recent Titles in
Contributions in Afro-American and African Studies
Series Adviser: Hollis R. Lynch

Africans and Seminoles: From Removal to Emancipation
Daniel F. Littlefield, Jr.

American Socialism and Black Americans: From the Age of Jackson to
World War II
Philip S. Foner

Black Academic Libraries and Research Collections: An Historical Survey
Jessie Carney Smith

The American Slave: A Composite Autobiography
Supplementary Series
George P. Rawick, editor

Trabelin' On: The Slave Journey to an Afro-Baptist Faith
Mechal Sobel

Revisiting Blassingame's *The Slave Community:* The Scholars Respond
Al-Tony Gilmore, editor

The "Hindered Hand": Cultural Implications of Early African-
American Fiction
Arlene A. Elder

The Cherokee Freedmen: From Emancipation to American Citizenship
Daniel F. Littlefield, Jr.

Teachers' Pets, Troublemakers, and Nobodies: Black Children in
Elementary School
Helen Gouldner

The Separate Problem: Case Studies of Black Education in the North,
1900–1930
Judy Jolley Mohraz

The Slave Drivers: Black Agricultural Labor Supervisors in the Antebellum South
William L. Van Deburg

THE BLACK RURAL LANDOWNER— ENDANGERED SPECIES
Social, Political, and Economic Implications

EDITED BY
Leo McGee and Robert Boone

Contributions in Afro-American and African Studies, Number 44

GREENWOOD PRESS

WESTPORT, CONNECTICUT • LONDON, ENGLAND

Library of Congress Cataloging in Publication Data
Main entry under title:
The Black rural landowner—endangered species.

(Contributions in Afro-American and African studies; 14 ISSN
0069–9624)
Includes bibliographical references and index.
1. Land tenure—Southern States—History. 2. Southern
States—Rural conditions. 3. Afro-Americans—Economic
conditions. I. McGee, Leo. II. Boone, Robert. III. Series.
HD207.B57   333.3'232   78–69538
ISBN 0–313–20609–0

Library of Congress Catalog Card Number: 78-69538
ISBN: 0-313-20609-0
ISSN: 0069-9624

First published in 1979

Greenwood Press, Inc.
51 Riverside Avenue, Westport, Connecticut 06880

Printed in the United States of America

10   9   8   7   6   5   4   3   2   1

CONTENTS

ILLUSTRATIONS

FIGURES

TABLES

ACKNOWLEDGMENTS

Many individuals have made significant contributions to the preparation of this book. Their support began at the conceptualization stage and continued through its completion.

Special appreciation is extended to Dr. Robert Boxley and Dr. Gene Wunderlich of the U.S. Department of Agriculture for assisting the editors in focusing on specific issues related to the black landowner.

The editors are eternally indebted to Dr. Carl Marbury for his immeasurable support. His keen insight, sensitivity, and dedication to the welfare of all mankind were perhaps the strongest ingredients that motivated and directed the editors throughout this endeavor. It is with gratitude that the editors acknowledge all who supported this effort.

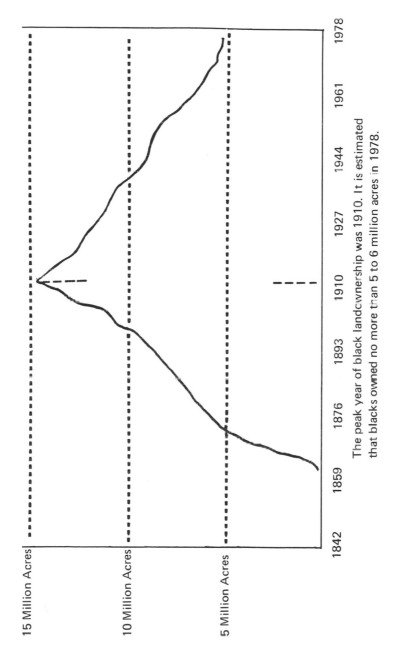

The peak year of black landownership was 1910. It is estimated that blacks owned no more than 5 to 6 million acres in 1978.

FIGURE 1   Accumulation and Decline of Black-Owned Rural Land

INTRODUCTION
Leo McGee and
Robert Boone

The economic status of this nation has depended greatly on the efficient utilization of farmland. A great proportion of farm labor supply has been provided by blacks. Throughout history, blacks have been closely attached to land, whether through field production or domestic service on farms or plantations.[1]

Following emancipation blacks engaged more vigorously in land-based pursuits, at first by agreeing to sharecrop with white landowners. It is estimated that by 1910, the peak year of black landownership in the United States, blacks owned 15 million acres. By 1920, the total number of farms operated by blacks was 926,000 and blacks comprised one-seventh of all farmers in the United States. Included in this number were tenant farmers who supplied all of the labor and exercised managerial functions while being paid with a share of the crop.[2]

Since the turn of the century, it is estimated that blacks have lost in excess of 9 million acres of rural land. The economic impact of this has not been fully comprehended by many Americans. It is reported that in the South land constitutes possibly the largest equity base under black control. The 5 to 6 million rural acres presently owned by blacks, primarily in the South, are valued at approximately $750 million.[3] This is the largest equity resource controlled by blacks in the South.

In the rural South, studies have indicated that landownership by blacks tends to correlate highly with characteristics generally regarded as worthy of encouragement within the black community. "Land owning blacks have proved to be more likely to register and to vote, and more likely to run for public office than non-landowners."[4] In effect, landownership gives blacks a measure of independence, a sense of security, and the dignity and power which are crucial to the elevation of the social and economic status of the black community.[5]

The impact of rural landownership by blacks transcends the actual monetary value of the land itself. Ownership of land positively affects one's psychological state, which may be more important particularly at a time when blacks are attempting to show greater signs of security and independence in determining their own destiny.

In 1935, the average size of a black-operated farm in the South was 44 acres; white farms averaged 131 acres. In 1959, the average white farm nearly doubled, rising to 249 acres. The average size of black farms in 1959 was 52 acres, an increase of just 8 acres since 1935.[6]

Since 1910, the amount of land owned by black farmers has steadily decreased with the exception of the period from 1940 to 1950. "During that one decade under the prosperous conditions of the War and immediate post war period, there was a growth in both the number of Negroes and farmers who owned land."[7]

Black migration to the North is one of the significant factors that has contributed to the precipitous decline in black landownership. Moreover, it is postulated that more recently thousands of blacks have sold acres of their land to make way for new industries, tourist facilities, and suburban development.[8]

In 1910, 91 percent of the nation's 9.8 million blacks lived in the South. Twenty-seven percent of American Negroes lived in cities of 2,500 persons or more, as compared to 48 percent of the nation's white population. By 1966, the Negro population had increased to 21.5 million and two significant geographic shifts had taken place. The proportion of Negroes living in the South had dropped to 55 percent and about 69 percent of all Negroes lived in metropolitan areas.[9]

Black migration began after the Civil War, and accelerated during World War I when jobs were created in the North. After the war, the Depression slowed migration; however, it boomed again after World War II. Poverty worked both to push blacks out of farming and to make the attractions of city life irresistible.

More than three million southern blacks migrated to the large urban centers of the North between 1940 and 1960. Although almost everyone assumed that the northward flow slowed down during the years of hope spawned by protests and changes of the 1960s, recent census figures show that 1.4 million blacks left the South between 1960 and 1970.[10.]

Within recent years a new phenomenon seems to be developing. There is evidence that a trend of "reverse black migration" is taking place. The deterioration of the quality of city life coupled with high crime rates, overcrowdedness, pollution, and unemployment have spurred thousands of black professionals as well as the unskilled to return south. For many it is a return home; for others who have never lived in the South, it is a move to a more comfortable environment and a search for better economic conditions. Between 1971 and 1973, 247,000 blacks moved south while only 166,000 moved out.[11] Upon their return, many blacks attempt to insure themselves a stake in the largest equity resource controlled by blacks in the South. Often, they immediately purchase rural plots, make secure their family farm, or attempt to reclaim once-owned family land.

Two major reports have been released dealing with the decline in black-owned rural land. In 1973, Robert Browne of the Black Economic Research Center in New York released a study titled *Only Six Million Acres: A Decline of Black Owned Land in the Rural South.* Another study, completed by Lester Salamon in 1974, is *Black Owned Land: Profile of Disappearing Equity Base.*

Browne and Salamon[12] state that the more than 12 million acres of land in the South owned in full or in part by blacks in 1950 had declined to less than 6 million by 1969. For the same period, the number of black full and part owners declined from 193,000 to less than 67,000. Salamon forecasts that there will come a time when there will be no landowning blacks in the South. However, Beale[13] suggests that the black-owned rural acreage will not drop below 4,500,000; he also feels that there might be an increase in the future.

The reasons for the decline of black landownership are complex and many. Browne lists seven reasons for its rapid decline:[14]

1. Tax sales: the taking of tax-delinquent property by the state and auctioning it off to the highest bidder.
2. Partition sales: the number of heirs and the size of property is such that it is physically impossible or impractical to actually divide. Therefore, property is sold to the highest bidder and proceeds are

divided among heirs in the proportion of their interest in the land.
3. Mortgage foreclosures: the loss of mortgaged property due to a delinquent debt.
4. Failure to write wills: results in devolution of property by intestacy. Therefore, one's defense of right to property is considerably weakened.
5. Landownership limitations placed on welfare recipients: generally, to receive welfare assistance, one must not have sufficient income and resources to provide reasonable subsistence compatible with decency and health and assessed value of property must not exceed a certain amount.
6. Eminent domain: the taking of private property for public use.
7. Voluntary sale: often, black landowners do not receive fair compensation for the sale of their property due to their lack of sophistication in real estate transactions. Also, due to the lack of financial resources and/or technical skills to transform land into a viable investment, landownership is often perceived to be a financial liability rather than an asset to poverty-stricken landowners because of the drain of his/her financial resources to pay mortgage and property taxes without any compensating benefits. Therefore, land might be abandoned and left idle or sold for a nominal fee.

A vast majority of blacks left the South to escape conditions of poverty. The fascination of big city life seduced many others. For whatever reasons, it is widely accepted that the millions of blacks who migrated from the South contributed significantly to the decline of black-owned rural land. On the other hand, it is also widely accepted that the less than altruistic behavior patterns of land officials contributed most to the loss of rural land by blacks.

Developing strategies to arrest the rapid decline of black-owned rural real estate has high priority in the black community. This book represents the first in depth exploration of the many issues surrounding the black landowner. It reviews the history of land accumulation, land loss, and the black farmer's survival off the land in rural America from the post-Civil War years; it offers a comprehensive land-retention model and projects the future course of the black rural landowner.

NOTES

1. Robert S. Browne, *Only Six Million Acres: A Decline of Black Owned Land in the Rural South* (New York: The Black Economic Research Center, 1973), p. 19.

2. Ibid. Also see Calvin L. Beale, "The Negro in American Agriculture," reprinted from the *American Negro Reference Book*, John P. Davis, ed. (Englewood Cliffs, N.J.: Prentice Hall, 1966), p. 170.

3. Lester M. Salamon, *Black Owned Land: Profile of Disappearing Equity Base* (Washington, D.C.: Office of Minority Business Enterprise, U.S. Department of Commerce, 1974), p. ii.

4. Browne, *Only Six Million Acres,* pp. 24–25.

5. Lester M. Salamon, "Family Assistance—The Stakes in the Rural South," *New Republic,* February 20, 1971, pp. 17–18.

6. Calvin L. Beale, "Migration Patterns of Minorities in the U.S.," *American Journal of Agriculture Economics,* December 1974, p. 179.

7. Ibid., p. 196.

8. "Blacks Struggle to Keep Little Land They Have Left," *New York Times,* December 7, 1972, p. 39.

9. *Report of the National Advisory Commission on Civil Disorder* (New York: New York Times Co., 1968), p. 237.

10. Lerone Bennett, Jr., "Old Illusions and the New South," *Ebony,* August 1971, p. 36.

11. *Newsweek,* March 25, 1974, p. 38.

12. Browne, *Only Six Million Acres,* p. 19, and Lester M. Salamon, *Black Owned Land,* p. ii.

13. Beale, "Negro in American Agriculture," p. 170.

14. Browne, *Only Six Million Acres,* p. 45

THE BLACK RURAL LANDOWNER— ENDANGERED SPECIES

chapter 1

THE LAND QUESTION IN HISTORICAL PERSPECTIVE: THE ECONOMICS OF POVERTY IN THE BLACKBELT SOUTH, 1865–1920

Manning Marable

POST-CIVIL WAR LAND TENURE

A central chapter in the history of black America involves the evolution of black agriculture and land tenure in the Blackbelt South. After the Civil War, four million black people, about half of whom lived on the cotton-producing plantations of Georgia, Alabama, and Mississippi, owned almost nothing except their own clothes, some agricultural tools, farm animals, and their own labor power. Their immediate prospects for economic survival during this period of heightened racial tensions, black code legislation, and Ku Klux Klan terrorism seemed bleak. But by 1910, a generation after Appomattox, blacks had seemingly succeeded in achieving a minor economic miracle in the Deep South. The number of black owner-operated farms that year was 212,972, almost double that of only twenty years before. A small, yet growing black petty bourgeoisie controlled important trades inside major cities. With the financial support of black-owned banks, black farmers were purchasing land on credit, speculating on the cotton market, and successfully competing with most small white farmers and tenants. After World War I, the number of black owner-operators of farms gradually declined; a black exodus grew to major proportions as black families abandoned agriculture. The story of tremendous black land acquisitions prior to 1910 and the immediate causes for Blackbelt land losses after World War I are largely obscured from the pages of black history.[1]

The historiographical emphasis placed upon black migrations from the Deep South and upon the ghetto experiences of subsequent generations neglects the fact that the vast majority of these people were farmers until the Great Depression of the 1930s. Most black people chose freely to live and work in the South after slavery. From the end of the Civil War through the 1870s there was an increase in black migration into such urban centers as Mobile, Macon, and Selma, Alabama. It is probable that "the city was a much safer place for the independent-minded freeman than many of the more remote rural areas where it was relatively easy for hostile whites to take the law into their own hands with little chance of exposure or prosecution."[2] The majority of black men, women, and children who left their homes chose to move into the Blackbelt rather than into southern cities, the Upper South, or the northern states. Many Blackbelt counties in Georgia and Alabama experienced a black population increase of up to 25 percent within ten years. Historian Peter Kolchin wrote that "hundreds of blacks left the mountain and Piedmont counties of northern and central Alabama and relocated in the heart of the cotton country."[3] Simultaneously, many whites left the Blackbelt for the Piedmont counties north of Atlanta and Huntsville. The reason for the sudden relocation of blacks toward the old cotton plantation region was primarily economic: almost all black men "expected the plantations of their ex-masters to be divided among them."[4] In many areas, whites feared the "widespread rumor of a Negro insurrection due to the idea" that the plantations were "going to be distributed among them."[5]

Unfortunately, the basic pattern of southern land tenure changed very little after 1865. With the defeat of the southern armies and the emancipation of almost four million former slaves, the prospects for fundamental economic change seemed to be realistic. Historian Peter Camejo noted that "the land of the richest 70,000 slaveholders and public lands in the hands of the ex-Confederate states totaled 394 million acres. To give one million black families 40 acres each only amounted to 40 million acres."[6] In 1869, there were 6,496,421 acres of public domain in Alabama, and 4,718,517 acres in Mississippi.[7] The class and caste structure which had been constructed upon the foundations of black slavery did not relinquish its hegemony over the remainder of society. W. E. B. Du Bois wrote: "The great black belt plantations . . . had hardly been disturbed by war. The barons ruling there, who dictated the policy of the state, were to the last degree reactionary."[8] The occupying Union army did little to rearrange economic relations between masters

and their former slaves, and southern whites of every class did everything in their power to resurrect the *ancien régime*. "Alarmed by the
sharp rise in the number of independent black farmers," many white
planters refused to sell property to blacks.[9] Blacks were able to buy
several thousand acres of land confiscated by the federal government in
Alabama, Mississippi, and other southern states, but much of this property was not as fertile as the Blackbelt.[10] During Reconstruction (1867-
1877), the Republican justices of the peace and courts often sided with
black farmers in legal disputes over property or wages. Generally, black
people's demands for land always exceeded its availability.[11]

The plantation system was severely shaken by the war and Reconstruction, but it was hardly destroyed. Between 1850 and 1880 there
was a significant increase in the number of farms in the Deep South and
a decrease in the average amount of acres per farming unit. In Mississippi the number of farms increased from 33,960 to 101,772, and the
average acreage declined from 308.9 acres to 155.8 acres. Alabama
farms increased from 41,964 to 135,864, and average acreage declined
from 289.2 acres to 138.8 acres. Georgia recorded the greatest change:
an increase from 51,759 farms in 1850 to 138,626 in 1880, and a
reduction in acreage from 440.9 to only 187.9.[12] Most of these new
farms were purchased by poor whites or yeomen farmers, many of
whom lived in the Piedmont or extreme southern Appalachians.
Through skill and determination, however, hundreds of thousands
of black men did purchase what land was available to them. According
to the statistics of the Georgia comptroller general, the 83,318 black
men who were registered to vote in 1874 owned 338,769 acres of land
valued at $1.2 million. Their taxable property was worth $6.2 million,
and virtually all had been slaves only a single decade before. Still, the
majority of black farmers, financially unable or not allowed to purchase
land, stuck to sharecropping as the best of the possible alternatives.[13] As
historian C. Vann Woodward reflected, "The lives of the overwhelming majority of Negroes were still circumscribed by the farm and plantation. The same was true of the white people, but the Negroes, with few
exceptions, were farmers without land."[14]

Despite the presence of thousands of new farms, the planter class still
controlled a huge percentage of the land in the South. In most counties,
the wealthiest 5 percent of all landowners controlled 40 percent of the
property or more. The upper tenth of all farmers owned from one-half to

two-thirds of all land in every county. Most planters had four to six
tenant families working their property. The dramatic changes in property relations had occurred without challenging the hegemony of the
wealthy, Bourbon planter elite. For the newly freed blacks this meant
that the social and political, as well as economic institutions of southern
life would continue to be dominated by their former slavemasters.[15]

The new economic relationship that replaced slavery in the Blackbelt
was termed sharecropping. Under a typical sharecropping agreement,
the black farmer rented several acres of land and paid the planter a
portion of his cotton crop, usually about one-half. Surprisingly, both the
landlords and the laborers preferred sharecropping to wage labor. The
planters initially desired a system where blacks labored for a period of
twelve months for a predetermined wage, but the acute shortage of
currency after the war made this impractical. Many black people considered sharecropping to be a partnership between themselves and their
former masters. Blacks were free to grow their own food without the
landlord's constant interference, and they were able to determine the
length of each individual workday for themselves. In most Blackbelt
counties the sharecropper occupied a higher social status than the wage
laborer. The planters gradually accepted sharecropping, and despite the
degree of independence it afforded blacks, the system was superior to
slavery as a means of extracting surplus value from black labor. The
planter forced the cropper to buy his own farming implements, seed,
and household goods on credit at outrageous prices. The planter
weighed and marketed his cotton after the growing season and kept all
records. Eventually, most white planters realized that the long-term
effects of sharecropping reinforced their hegemony over black labor in a
more subtle yet permanent manner.[16]

Throughout the period, the major crop black farmers grew was cotton. King Cotton had breathed life into the nearly moribund body of
slavery at the beginning of the nineteenth century. The crop was the
economic staple for the frontier southern states of Mississippi,
Louisiana, Arkansas, and Alabama. The pattern of black antebellum life
evolved around the annual cycle of cotton production. "The picking
season must have struck the slaves as a mixed affair," historian Eugene
D. Genovese wrote. "It meant hard and distasteful work and sometimes
punishment for failure to meet quotas. . . ."[17] Du Bois observed that
the liberated slaves and their former masters returned to cotton as their

major, and too often, sole means of survival. "By 1870," Du Bois noted, "the cotton crop of Georgia had surpassed the largest crop raised under slavery."[18] Few farmers were overly concerned with the disastrous aspects and long-range problems involved with monocrop agriculture. Historians Gilbert C. Fite and Ladd Haystead wrote in their review of southern agriculture that "nobody worried about building a better diet. It was easier to grow only a cash crop, cotton, and then buy from the North much of the sketchy foods which were necessary."[19] The entire Blackbelt continued to depend upon cotton even after sharp decreases in its market price after the 1870s. So permanently scarred was the Blackbelt by its backward mode of agricultural production that life and labor patterns well into the 1900s seemed timeless. As late as 1944, sociologist Gunnar Myrdal in his epic study, *An American Dilemma*, could write that "in the main, cotton is cultivated by a primitive labor consuming agriculture technique which has not changed much since slavery."[20]

Black sharecroppers and owner-operators of small farms had little knowledge of the scientific farming techniques essential for the rapidly depleted soil of their region. The production of cotton year after year robbed the earth of important minerals. As early as the 1850s, many southern farmers realized that commercial fertilizers were essential for restoring the soil, but few acted upon this knowledge. Tidewater planters in Virginia and Maryland frequently used guano and marl.[21] Guano sold for $40 a ton and 450 to 900 pounds were needed to restore a single acre. Agricultural journals of the antebellum era commented frequently that Mississippi farmers refused to use either guano or marl, and planters in Alabama and Georgia applied it incorrectly by not using enough to make a real difference. Some Blackbelt planters used cottonseed to fertilize their corn crops, but relied on barnyard manure for their cotton fields.[22] Manure fertilizing demands meticulous storage as well as care in application. About 400 tons were needed to restore one exhausted acre. Genovese reported, and manure cost $2 per ton in 1850.[23] After emancipation, black owner-operators had no extensive experience in applying guano and marl and very few could even afford it.

Crop rotation on a planned basis would have aided black farmers in producing larger yields. But general scientific methods of planting and rotation, commonly practiced in the North, were used infrequently in the Blackbelt. Few small farmers realized that closely spaced cotton plants, which appeared to maximize the yield per acre, actually reduced the amount of cotton. High-density planting adversely affects the size of cotton bolls, plant height, and stem diameter. Without uniform plant distribution and careful hoeing, techniques about which the former slaves knew little, the total cotton yield became smaller and smaller with each consecutive growing season.[24] Farmers had known that annual crop rotation helped to restore their soil, but the overwhelming majority did not rotate with legumes (plants that would have returned needed nitrogen to the soil). Most alternated cotton with corn, a system that retarded soil depletion and erosion but did absolutely nothing to prevent it.[25]

Across the board, blacks who rented, sharecropped, or owned property planted a greater percentage of cotton than did white farmers. White owner-operators on the average planted 44.8 percent of their acreage in cotton, while black owner-operators planted 51.9 percent in cotton; black renters planted more than 60 percent of their land in cotton. The average white farmer planted three or four different crops, in addition to cotton, and devoted an average of 10.1 percent of his tilled acreage to crops other than cotton and corn combined. Black farmers seldom planted anything except cotton and corn. On the average, only 3.7 percent of black farmlands were planted in some other crop. The soil on black-owned farms therefore declined in productivity and value at a much faster rate than normal.[26] The domination of cotton led to a real decline in food production throughout the South. The per capita production of corn in 1870 fell to less than one-half the level of 1850, and remained there for several decades. The per capita production of swine dropped from 2.11 in 1850 to .73 in 1890; per capita production of sheep fell from .47 to .22. The decline in agricultural and livestock productivity was offset by the overproduction of cotton.[27]

Black farmers were caught within a poverty cycle which was almost impossible to transcend. In 1880, for example, the number of acres of cropland per worker on an average farm was 12.4 for white-owned farms and 7.5 for black-owned farms. Black sharecroppers averaged 8 acres per farmworker, while owner-operated black farms tended to be somewhat smaller, 6.6 acres per worker. Economists Roger Ransom and Richard Sutch, in their extensive study of southern agriculture, *One Kind of Freedom,* assert that the inequality of acreage per farmworker had numerous economic consequences for blacks. Black farmers were forced to cultivate crops on a significantly larger portion of their property every year than were whites. The ratio of uncultivated acres per cultivated acre on black small family farms was only .63 acres, but 2.72 acres on white owner-operated farms. The ratio of uncultivated acres per cultivated acre for black sharecroppers was only .34 acres. Ransom and Sutch estimate that more than one-third of all white owner-operators of small farms regularly purchased fertilizer, but only one-fifth of all black farmers could afford to do this. Without sufficient capital to pay for commercial fertilizers, black farmers relied upon their animals' manure to fertilize their crops. However, the average black farmer owned 1.3 work animals and only 5.2 swine, compared to 1.9 work animals and 9.9 swine owned by white farmers. This shortage of animals meant an insufficient supply of barnyard manure, which lowered agricultural yields, promoted soil erosion, and depleted the soil of nitrogen. Since sharecroppers traditionally gave half of their annual crop to their landlords, it becomes clear that the exploitation of slavery continued to be present within the new form of economic relations. "Emancipation removed the legal distinction between the South's two races, but it left them in grossly unequal economic positions," Ransom and Sutch noted. "Black farmers had less capital, smaller farms," and were "more susceptible to exploitation."[28]

The entire cotton-producing South was extremely rural and existed, in effect, as a domestic colony for the remainder of the nation. In 1880 there were only three cities in the Blackbelt that had both a population in excess of fifteen thousand people and five banks—Montgomery, Atlanta, and Memphis. Jackson, the capital city of Mississippi, was a sleepy, conservative hamlet of barely five thousand people. Athens, the former capital of Georgia, was a more prosperous village of 6,100, possessing two banks, twenty general stores, and the state's university. Other than that, the Blackbelt was overwhelmingly agricultural, its towns sparsely populated and culturally backward. Town merchants came to dominate both the flow of trade and the relative accessibility of credit, due to the general lack of banking facilities. Several important towns, such as Tuskegee with a population of almost 2,500 in 1880, had no bank at all. Tuskegee's merchant class operated the town's sixteen general stores and was responsible for supplying credit to all farmers and planters, giving them canned goods, fine cloth, flour, sugar, seed, and farm equipment in the winter and early spring of each year in return for a promised share of the farmers' fall profits. This pattern of a merchant-dominated economy occurred in county after county. In Selma, Alabama's third largest city, there were only two banks but twenty general stores, all in the active business of making short-term loans to cotton planters and sharecroppers. Cotton-producing communities such as Demopolis, Alabama, Albany, Georgia, and Greenville, Mississippi, each having only one bank, required the lending services and continued support of their merchant classes.[29]

County merchants were charged anywhere from 3 to 15 percent interest by wholesale merchants and suppliers for their goods. The local merchants not only passed these expenses along to rural consumers, but made a prosperous living by extending credit for periods of less than one year at extraordinarily high rates. An average Georgia merchant in 1889 would have charged 66 cents for one bushel of corn purchased in cash, but would charge 87 cents for the same corn if purchased on credit. The average cash price for a pound of bacon in Georgia that same year, $7.91, was much lower than the credit price of $10.38. During the 1880s the average interest rates charged by Georgia merchants for one pound of bacon and one bushel of corn paid four months after initial purchase were 88.9 percent and 92.8 percent, respectively. In several years, the interest rate for the purchase of corn exceeded 120 percent for a four-month period. Part of the reason for these exorbitant rates was that the majority of communities in the Blackbelt contained only one or two stores within a radius of ten or fifteen miles. Sometimes an affluent merchant would purchase property and become a landlord or manager of sharecroppers; occasionally, the planters themselves went into the grocery store business. Generally, a single owner of a store or group of stores developed a small but tight monopoly for himself at the expense of poor farmers and tenants in the county.[30]

Black sharecroppers and small planters alike depended upon the rural merchants in the country stores throughout the region to extend them adequate credit for each growing season. During dry seasons or in the winter, farmers often borrowed on their next year's crops, purchasing items that they could not pay for without credit. These county merchants who were often in debt to their regional suppliers and investors were in a position to demand that only crops producing a sure profit could be planted. In practical terms, the merchants insisted that cotton be grown at the expense of any other staple, since cotton had always brought a handsome profit on the market. As a result, many black farmers who might have planted corn or other vegetables for their families were forced to grow cotton and purchase some of their food at the country store. These farming practices further depleted the soil and led to annual reductions in yields. Most important, the overproduction of cotton caused by merchants' demands depressed the market price of cotton. From 1865 until 1898 the price of cotton declined steadily: from 29 cents per pound in 1868, to 11 cents per pound in 1890, to about 5 cents in 1898. It cost roughly 7 cents per pound just to grow cotton, excluding any profit.[31]

Cotton's monopoly across the Blackbelt made millions of dollars for white planters, affluent merchants, businessmen, and cotton market speculators. As long as the world demand for cotton was high, the impetus for establishing alternative staples in agriculture was low. Cotton's monopoly also degraded black and white labor, depleted the soil, and concentrated the bulk of the best farmland in the hands of a racist, class-conscious aristocracy. "For the South as a whole, cotton specialization was not more profitable than diversified economy with a balance between agriculture and industry," Ransom and Sutch asserted. "The curse of King Cotton was the lack of prosperity he imposed upon the South."[32]

ECONOMIC SELF-SUFFICIENCY

The development of a number of small, black-owned banks and lending institutions helped to transform the poverty of black life in the South. During the 1880s a small number of determined black ministers, entrepreneurs, and educators pooled their resources to begin savings banks for blacks in several southern cities. The Reverend W.R. Pettiford, pastor of the Sixteenth Street Colored Baptist Church, started the Alabama Penny Savings Bank in Birmingham and gradually opened branch offices in Montgomery, Anniston, and Selma. Booker T. Washington, principal of Tuskegee Institute, initiated a savings department at the college which functioned as a local bank. In the first decade of the twentieth century dozens of black banks were established which loaned thousands of dollars to poor black farming families, desperately attempting to compete within a demanding marketplace. By 1911 there were seven black-owned banks in Alabama and two in Georgia. Mississippi boasted eleven such banks located in Jackson (two), Vicksburg (two), Yazoo City, Columbus, Greenville, Mound Bayou, Indianola, Natchez, and Shaw. These black-owned banks and forty-two others throughout the country did an annual business of $20 million in 1910.[33]

The rise of literacy tremendously aided prospects for black rural development. Immediately after slavery ended 90 percent of all black people over twenty years of age were unable to read and write. As planters maintained all records and county merchants kept credit records, it was likely that many if not all blacks were cheated on a regular basis. The creation of primary and secondary schools and agricultural colleges gradually lowered illiteracy rates, especially among the younger blacks. By 1890 about one-half of all blacks between the ages of ten and nineteen were literate. As illiteracy diminished below 50 percent after 1900, a greater number of black people were able to compete for jobs requiring a minimal education. Black people across the Blackbelt were aware that literacy and an aptitude in basic mathematics would make them more self-sufficient and ultimately more in command of their own lives.[34]

The development of a strong black land base became an ideological imperative of black thought by the 1890s. Throughout the Blackbelt, black farmers organized small agricultural fairs, exhibiting and selling swine, cows, sheep, and other livestock, vegetables, and cotton. The Agricultural and Mechanical College for Negroes was established in Normal, Alabama, in 1875, where many black students learned the essentials of crop rotation, proper fertilization techniques, and other skills necessary for progressive farming. With the financial support of northern philanthropic agencies and churches, dozens of black agricultural and teachers' training colleges were established. The largest and most influential institutions included the Georgia State Industrial College in Savannah, Knox Academy in Selma, Tuskegee Institute, Haines Normal and Industrial Institute in Augusta, Utica Normal and Industrial School in Utica, Mississippi, and the State Normal School in Montgomery. W.H. Holtzclaw, the principal of Utica Institute, established a company which purchased plantations for resale to black sharecroppers. Most of these schools held yearly farmers' conferences, and many offered monthly training institutes on advanced agricultural techniques. Within a single generation, thousands of young black men were trained to become more competent in the agricultural sciences than any white plantation owner had ever been. It was, of course, only a beginning. However, proper education and a gradually improving economic climate enabled young black graduates from these small institutions to compete with white owner-operators on a more equal basis.[35]

Booker T. Washington was perhaps the most influential advocate of Blackbelt agricultural development. Better known as the architect of the "Atlanta Compromise" of 1895 which acquiesced to the emergence of segregation and white racism, Washington was actually a complex and ambitious man. Always the pragmatist, he sensed the shift in the political winds and responded accordingly, issuing ambiguous statements which appeased white racists while guaranteeing a continued flow of funds into his college and other black educational institutions. From the founding of Tuskegee Institute in 1881, Washington was a strong advocate of scientific farming and increased black land tenure. Students at Tuskegee cultivated sweet potatoes, corn, peas, okra, and vegetables of all kinds for consumption and sale from the institute's farm.[36] Through Washington's subtle political initiatives and compromises, hundreds of black farmers became successful in their efforts to buy land. In 1900, 157 black farmers in Macon County owned land; by 1910, the number increased to 507. Tuskegee graduates established "social settlements" in a sharecropping area of Lowndes County, Alabama, purchasing old plantation property and reselling it to eager black farmers.[37] Washington remained convinced that a rural black petty bourgeois elite of farmers, small bankers, and merchants could form the basis for a black economy inside American capitalism. In a lecture titled "How To Build a Race" given at the institute's chapel on a Sunday night in October 1898, Washington described in detail the problem of black agricultural underdevelopment and possible solutions:

> We are living in a country where, if we are going to succeed at all we are going to do so by what we raise out of the soil. Without this no people can succeed. No race which fails to put brains into agriculture can succeed; and if you want to realize the truth of this statement go with me this month into the back districts of Georgia, Mississippi and Alabama and you will find these people almost in a starving condition, slowly starving to death and yet they are surrounded by a rich country. Are you going to stand still

and see these people starve? Are you not willing to make any
sacrifice in order to prepare yourselves to help these people? I
believe you will learn all you can about agriculture and about the
use of improved machinery.

Washington warned his students that agricultural development was
"our only (hope for) salvation as a race."[38]

A substantial petty bourgeoisie slowly began to take shape—black
undertakers, grocery store owners, tailors, insurance men, and bankers.
In Atlanta a number of the city's most prosperous contractors and build-
ers were black entrepreneurs; in Charleston blacks controlled the city's
barbering and butchering trades. According to the statistics of the National Negro Business League, between 1900 and 1914 the number of
black-owned drug stores increased from 250 to 695; black undertaking
firms grew from 450 to 1,000; the number of black retail merchants
increased from 10,000 to 25,000. Individual examples of black
economic self-sufficiency and success existed in every major southern
city and in many rural counties. R.R. Church of Memphis quietly
accumulated real estate in that city and by the early 1900s was worth
approximately one million dollars. Charles Banks, a leading citizen of
the all-black community of Mound Bayou, established a cottonseed oil
mill, a loan and investment company, and a bank. Many of these black
entrepreneurs shared Washington's philosophy of racial pride and his
faith in the capitalist system.[39]

As economic conditions improved in the early 1900s, the prospects
for Booker T. Washington's vision of a self-sufficient black economy
seemed increasingly realistic. Despite a general decline in cotton prices,
there was an increase in southern industrial output. The number of
cotton mills increased from 161 in 1880 to 400 in 1900, the greatest
increase coming during the 1890-1900 period. Capital investments in
cotton mills soared from $17.4 million to $124.6 million between 1880
and 1900. During the same twenty years, the number of cottonseed oil
mills increased from 45 to 353.[40] By 1908 coal production in north-
central Alabama had increased three times over the amount produced
in 1890. Thousands of black sharecroppers abandoned the land temporarily or permanently to work in Birmingham's rich coal mines.[41] Increased
industrialization of the South, combined with a rapid rise in cotton prices
after 1898, made farming a profitable venture once more.

Black farmers succeeded in buying millions of acres of land which had previously been unavailable to them. Between 1900 and 1910 Carolina blacks purchased more than one million acres of farmland. Thousands of sharecroppers and tenant farmers in Mississippi, Alabama, and Georgia were able to purchase their own farms and compete with poorer white farmers. As Washington predicted boldly in 1898, "the vast unoccupied lands in the South . . . are simply waiting for those with capital, foresight and faith to step in and occupy."[42]

Virtually all economists agree with the observation of Richard T. Ely and George S. Wehrwein that black land tenure "in the South reached its peak in 1910."[43] There were 2,143,176 black farmers in 1911, a few of whom were just as prosperous and efficient as the most wealthy white landlords. Deal Jackson of Albany, Georgia, a former slave, owned more than 2,000 acres of rich farmland and held "forty (black) families" as tenants "on his plantation." Georgia blacks owned property worth $34 million and possessed 1,639,919 acres of land.[44] The thirst for land was so great within the black rural South that some blacks migrated directly to communities where there was an immediate "history of lynchings and mob violence, so long as land could be purchased at low prices."[45] "For a decade the cotton belt had enjoyed a happy conjunction of rising production and rising prices," historian George B. Tindall wrote in *The Emergence of the New South*. "On the eve of (World War I) cotton fetched thirteen cents a pound, and a bumper crop of more than sixteen million bales, the largest yet known, was being laid to ripen."[46] About two-thirds of this amount was exported to Europe.[47] In these flush times, black people acquired the largest amount of property they would ever own within the United States. In 1910, there were approximately 175,000 farms fully owned by blacks, 43,000 partially owned, and 670,000 sharecropped. There were also one thousand black managers and supervisors of farm property. Blacks operated 890,000 farms and had become the proud owners of more than 15 million acres of land. In the late summer of 1914, Washington's dream of a flourishing black economy in the South seemed to be on the verge of reality.[48]

DECLINE OF BLACK AGRICULTURE AND LAND TENURE

The outbreak of World War I marked the beginning of the long and tragic decline of black agriculture and land tenure in the South. European nations which had been the largest consumers of cotton closed their doors to transatlantic commerce for about three months. All farmers were forced to sell their cotton to speculators at 5 to 8 cents per pound, well below current market value. Many struggling black farmers hauled their cotton into town and learned to their amazement that no one would buy it at any price. Southern politicians and regional capitalists realized that immediate steps had to be taken to help cotton producers, but most of the assistance went to white planters and merchants. Senator John H. Bankhead of Alabama proposed that his state extend $40 million worth of credit to farmers and store their cotton in state warehouses. Asa G. Candler, Atlanta millionaire and a director of the Coca Cola company, offered low-interest loans to white planters and stored one-quarter of a million bales of cotton in his huge warehouses. Within two months, southern farmers lost about $500 million. The 1913 average farm price for cotton was not achieved until June 1916, when drastic cuts in the amount of cotton produced created an artificially high price.[49] The cotton disaster of 1914 ruined many thousands of black and white farmers, and affected southern agriculture for years to come. As bourgeois economist John Kenneth Galbraith observed, "Unlike most industry, agriculture is peculiarly incapable of dealing with the problems of expanding output and comparatively inelastic demand."[50]

Black farmers who borrowed money to purchase their land suddenly had no way to pay annual mortgage payments and notes of credit. Sharecroppers who owned no property were not as threatened with sudden economic collapse as were black small owner-operators. However, both groups had no experience in growing any money crop other than cotton, and many desperate county merchants refused to allow blacks additional credit to plant anything except cotton. In the summer of 1916, severe rainstorms destroyed much of that year's cotton crop throughout Alabama and Mississippi. Robert R. Moton, then principal of Tuskegee Institute, informed the U.S. Department of Agriculture and Alabama state officials in September of that year that many black farmers "have grown discontented because of lack of the most ordinary necessities." He pleaded for seed and agricultural supplies "so that they could have something growing, [and so] that many of them would be contented and not be inclined to leave the farm."[51] Making matters worse, many black banks were forced out of business with the collapse of the cotton market. By 1918, only one black-owned-and-operated bank remained in Alabama, the savings office of Tuskegee Institute.

Only two black banks existed in Mississippi, in Mound Bayou and Indianola. With the failure of these financial institutions, a significant source of credit disappeared.[52] Many thousands of farmers sold their land for only a fraction of its real value to pay off mounting debts. Black sharecroppers who might have planned to buy land and sell their own cotton crops on the open market were certainly discouraged from doing so. My great grandfather, Morris Marable, was an independent farmer in Randolph County, Alabama, who operated his own cotton gin and marketed four or five bales of his cotton crop each year. With the reduction of the price of cotton, he was forced out of the market. In several years he abandoned agriculture entirely, like thousands of other black farmers and small entrepreneurs.

More destructive than the impact of the war upon cotton prices was the coming of the boll weevil. Entering from Mexico and Central America into southern Texas, it spread across the state within ten years, destroying thousands of acres of cotton. By 1908 it had crossed the Mississippi and was ruining cotton fields along the rich, black delta country. The weevil, unlike other insects or worms, was especially difficult to detect until damage was already done. The adult female weevil lays her eggs in the fruit of the plant during the spring. When the eggs hatch in late summer the young eat the cotton.

By 1916 every county in Alabama was infested with boll weevils and by 1920 every Georgia county reported insect damage. In each state in the Deep South, the boll weevil limited the number of acres planted as well as the normal yield of cotton lint in pounds per acre. In the four years preceding boll weevil infestation in Georgia, for example, an average of 4,953,000 acres of cotton were planted; four years after complete infestation, an average of 3,476,000 acres were planted with cotton, a reduction of almost 30 percent. The average yield of cotton lint per acre in Georgia was 230 pounds before infestation; after the insect's appearance, the average yield was reduced to 117 pounds, a decline of 49 percent.[53] Blackbelt farmers reduced the cotton acreage planted and because of the pests, they obtained approximately one-fifth to one-half less cotton lint per acre. Few sharecroppers and black owner-operators could afford expensive insecticides or poisons, and it was almost impossible to contain the spread of the insects. ''Field after field of cotton was eaten away,'' Haystead and Fite wrote. Some farms were spontaneously ''abandoned.''[54]

Compounding the economic troubles of black farmers was a general worsening of race relations in the Blackbelt. Those blacks who continued to vote after 1900 found that virtually every major or minor white political tendency in the Deep South, whether Democratic, Populist, or Republican, had repudiated the principle of black suffrage. In northern Alabama, black Republicans published the *Huntsville Republican* and attempted to organize support for whites who sympathized with Negro rights. By 1902 the Republican Lily White faction succeeded in purging the integrated Black and Tan group from the state convention by placing armed guards at the doors to keep blacks out. Within the decade, Black and Tan Republicanism was dead in Mississippi and Alabama.[55] After World War I, Alabama blacks organized suffrage leagues and initiated court challenges to *de jure* segregation, but most cases failed at the local level. During the 1920s neither the conservative nor the progressive factions of the Democratic party sought to expand the slender black electorate. The number of black voters in Alabama declined from a statewide total of 3,742 in 1908 to 1,500 in 1930.[56] For practical purposes, the Fifteenth Amendment no longer existed in the Blackbelt. Georgia led the nation in lynchings between 1885 and 1918 with 398. Mississippi was a close second with 381 and Alabama was fifth with 246. In 1915 there were 18 lynchings in Georgia alone, twice as many as in any other state. Appropriately, both Mississippi and Alabama were tied for second place that year with 9 illegal hangings of black people.[57] Carter G. Woodson, reviewing the economic chaos which had befallen black farmers throughout the South, refused to attribute the exodus of blacks to the North to any but political reasons. "It is highly probable that the Negroes would not be leaving the South today," the Negro historian wrote in 1918, "if they were treated as men."[58]

Facing economic disaster, most white farmers had sufficient resources to change the production habits of a century. Thousands of white farmers began to purchase and raise cattle. In Mississippi the number of cattle and calves produced rose from 873,356 in 1900 to 1,250,479 in 1920. Georgia cattle production went from 899,491 in 1900 to 1,156,738 in 1920.[59] Farmers in the pine hills and wire grass country of southern Georgia and southeast Alabama discovered that their red soil was excellent for peanuts, and peanut production increased during the 1920s and 1930s.[60] Whites borrowed heavily to maintain their land, and by crop diversification and decreased production of cotton, they were usually able to stay in business. Black farmers, several years behind in debts, could do little else except abandon their property and go into sharecropping, or leave their outstanding debts and flee to the North. Many chose the second option. From 1880 to 1910, only 79,400 blacks left the Blackbelt for the North; between 1910 and 1920, the figure leaped to 226,900, and from 1920 to 1930 about 444,400 black migrants fled the Deep South. Most if not all of these people were sharecroppers, small owner-operators, or workers in jobs connected with agriculture.[61]

There are many reasons which explain in part the demise of black land tenure in the Blackbelt South, and the destruction of an authentic, black landowning class. Several causes have been isolated—the emergence of white racism and Jim Crow legislation, the fall of cotton prices, the coming of the boll weevil, the lack of adequate credit at reasonable rates, the general erosion and depletion of the soil. All of these reasons and others stem from a larger and as yet unanswered dilemma—the existence and survival of black people within the context of the American capitalist system. In theory, capitalism is characterized by a degree of labor mobility and a free movement of capital from disadvantageous enterprises to more profitable sectors. However, under the economic conditions of the capitalist system prevalent in the post-bellum South, an elite group of white planters, bankers, investors, and merchants held a tight monopoly over the monetary supply, credit sources and rates, and the entire agricultural production of the region. Millions of poor white and black farmers were forced to supply an international market with cotton at the expense of building a viable industrial base within the South. This economic monopoly gradually promoted the collapse of the black economic miracle which black educators and entrepreneurs such as Booker T. Washington dreamed of building. Given the structure of the domestic economy, it was inevitable that black farmers would be forced off the land and evicted from their homes to work at factory jobs in the cities of the New South and the urban ghettos of the North.

As economist Paul Sweezy observed critically in *The Theory of Capitalist Development,* ''the very essence of monopoly is the existence of effective barriers to [the] free movement of capital.''[62] Neither the white South's social institutions, corrupted from the bottom up by racist ideology and violence, nor its electoral political institutions, which actually represented roughly one-fifth of the entire adult population, could provide fundamental solutions to the region's regressive economic order. History illustrates clearly that the goal of black economic self-sufficiency within the framework of the existing capitalist system is a bitter illusion rather than a possibility; the collapse of black land tenure in the Blackbelt South was not a failure of black people, but a failure of the state and private enterprise to promote equality of economic opportunity for all members of the society.

NOTES

1. John Hope Franklin, *From Slavery to Freedom* (New York: Alfred A. Knopf, third edition, 1969), p. 398. This essay defines the Blackbelt as those counties in Georgia, Alabama, Mississippi, South Carolina, and Louisiana that contained a percentage of black people in excess of 50 percent of the county's total population and depended upon cotton as their primary agricultural product between 1865 and 1910. In 1880, about 5.5 million people lived in the Blackbelt, including 3 million black people. These counties produced 4.1 million bales of cotton in 1880, almost three-fourths of the South's total production.

2. Peter Kolchin, *First Freedom: The Responses of Alabama's Blacks to Emancipation and Reconstruction* (Westport, Conn.: Greenwood Press, 1972), pp. 10– 11.

3. Ibid., pp. 12– 19.

4. Ibid., p 16.

5. W.E.B. Du Bois, *Black Reconstruction in America, 1860-1880* (New York: Russell & Russell, 1935), p. 434; Lawanda Cox, "Promise Land for the Freedman," *Mississippi Valley Historical Review* 45 (December 1958), pp. 418– 40. A Marxian perspective of southern blacks' desires for land after Reconstruction is presented in Manuel Gottlieb, "The Land Question in Georgia during Reconstruction," *Science and Society* 3 (Summer 1939), pp. 356– 88.

6. Peter Camejo, *Racism, Revolution and Reaction, 1861-1877: The Rise and Fall of Radical Reconstruction* (New York: Monad Press, 1976), p. 52.

7. Herbert Aptheker, ed., *A Documentary History of the Negro People in the United States* (New York: Citadel Press, 1951), pp. 627, 633– 36.

8. Du Bois, *Black Reconstruction,* p. 431. For many years, Du Bois was interested in rural economic development in the South. As early as 1893, while a doctoral student at the University of Berlin, Du Bois had composed a paper on the subject, "Die Landwirtschaftliche Entwickelung inden Sudstaaten der Vereinigten Staaten." Du Bois to the Trustees of the John F. Slater Fund, December 6, 1893, in Herbert Aptheker, ed., *The Correspondence of W.E.B. Du*

Bois, vol. 1 (Amherst, Mass.: University of Massachusetts Press, 1973), pp. 26–27.

9. Lerone Bennett, Jr., *Black Power, U.S.A.: The Human Side of Reconstruction, 1867-1877* (Chicago: Johnson Publishing Company, 1967), p. 332.

10. Franklin, *From Slavery to Freedom,* p. 312.

11. Bennett, *Black Power, U.S.A.,* p. 331.

12. Ladd Haystead and Gilbert C. Fite, *The Agricultural Regions of the United States* (Norman, Okla.: Oklahoma University Press, 1955), pp. 110–11.

13. Du Bois, *Black Reconstruction,* p. 508.

14. C. Vann Woodward, *Origins of the New South, 1877-1913* (Baton Rouge, La.: Louisiana State University Press, 1951), p. 205.

15. Roger Ransom and Richard Sutch, *One Kind of Freedom: The Economic Consequences of Emancipation* (New York: Cambridge University Press, 1977), pp. 77–80.

16. August Meier and Elliott Rudwick, *From Plantation to Ghetto* (New York: Hill & Wang Press, revised edition, 1976), pp. 171–72, 173; Kolchin, *First Freedom,* pp. 41–42; Joseph D. Reid, Jr., "Sharecropping as an Understandable Market Response," *Journal of Economic History* 33 (March 1973), pp. 106–30; Joseph D. Reid, Jr., "Sharecropping in History and Theory," *Agricultural History* 49 (April 1975), pp. 426–40. One of the earliest histories of tenancy is E.A. Goldenweiser and Leon Truesdell, *Farm Tenancy in the United States* (College Station, Tex.: Texas A & M University Press, 1921). Influential studies on sharecropping during the Great Depression include Charles S. Johnson, Edwin R. Embree, and W.W. Alexander, *The Collapse of Cotton Tenancy* (Chapel Hill, N.C.: University of North Carolina Press, 1935), and David Eugene Conrad, *The Forgotten Farmers* (Urbana, Ill.: University of Illinois Press, 1965).

17. Eugene D. Genovese, *Roll, Jordan, Roll: The World the Slaves Made* (New York: Pantheon Books, 1974), p. 322.

18. Du Bois, *Black Reconstruction,* p. 510.

19. Haystead and Fite, *The Agricultural Regions of the United States,* p. 106.

20. Gunnar Myrdal, *An American Dilemma* (New York: Harper & Brothers, 1944), p. 233. Cotton's central place in the South's economic history is reviewed in Gavin Wright, "Cotton Competition and the Post-Bellum Recovery of the American South," *Journal of Economic History* 34 (September 1974), pp. 610–35; David L. Cohn, *The Life and Times of King Cotton* (New York: Oxford University Press, 1956).

21. Guano is a substance consisting largely of seafowl excrement or cannery waste. Marl is a sandy, loose earth deposit, containing a large amount of calcium carbonate ($CaCO_3$).

22. Cottonseed is the seed of the cotton plant. When crushed, it makes a rich oil which is sometimes used in the preparation of protein meal.

23. On fertilization in southern agriculture, see Eugene D. Genovese, *The Political Economy of Slavery* (New York: Pantheon Books, 1965), pp. 90–95, and Rosser H. Taylor, "The Sale and Application of Commercial Fertilizers in the South Atlantic States," *Agricultural History* 21 (January 1947), pp. 46–52. Common antebellum agricultural practices and problems in farming are the subject of Keith Aufhauser's essay, "Slavery and Scientific Management," *Journal of Economic History* 33 (December 1973), pp. 811–23.

24. J. L. Fowler and L. L. Ray, "Response of Two Cotton Genotypes to Five Equidistant Spacing Patterns," *Agronomy Journal* 69 (September-October 1977), p. 733.

25. Genovese, *The Political Economy of Slavery*, pp. 96–97.

26. Ransom and Sutch, *One Kind of Freedom*, p. 185.

27. Ibid., pp. 150–54; Stephen J. DeCanio, "Cotton 'Overproduction' in Late Nineteenth Century Southern Agriculture," *Journal of Economic History* 33 (September 1973), pp. 608–33.

28. Ransom and Sutch, *One Kind of Freedom*, pp. 182–85.

29. Ibid., pp. 300–5.

30. Ibid., pp. 140–48; Glenn N. Sisk, "Rural Merchandising in the Alabama Black Belt, 1875–1917," *Journal of Farm Economics* 37 (November 1955), pp. 705–15.

31. Jack T. Kirby, *Darkness at the Dawning: Race and Reform in the Progressive South* (Philadelphia: Lippincott, 1972), p. 8.

32. Ransom and Sutch, *One Kind of Freedom*, pp. 190–91. The position of black people within the total capitalist economic structure is presented in Robert Higgs, *Competition and Coercion: Blacks in the American Economy, 1865-1914* (New York: Cambridge University Press, 1977).

33. Monroe Work, *Negro Year Book and Annual Encyclopedia of the Negro* (Tuskegee Institute: Tuskegee Institute Press, 1912), pp. 22, 168, 176, 177, 178. The emergence of the black entrepreneur within the South is skillfully documented in Du Bois's essay, "The Economic Revolution in the South," in Booker T. Washington and W.E.B. Du Bois, *The Negro in the South* (Philadelphia: G. W. Jacobs & Co., 1907).

34. Ransom and Sutch, *One Kind of Freedom*, p. 30.

35. Work, *Negro Year Book*, pp. 17, 110, 114–18; Kilby, *Darkness at the Dawning*, p. 173. The Morrill Act of 1890 created segregated schools for black agricultural students in seventeen states. Interestingly enough, this racist legislation has never been changed, and existing legislation affecting black agricultural education has been codified upon it. In 1971, for example, of the $76.8 million in U.S. Department of Agriculture funds which were allocated to agricultural

colleges in the states which established segregated school systems, 95.5 percent of the funds went to white schools; $28.8 million marked for agricultural research and forestry research in 1971 was received by white southern colleges; not one penny was granted to black colleges that year for research. See David Dyar Massey, "The Federation of Southern Cooperatives: Hard Times and High Hopes," *Southern Exposure* 2 (Autumn 1974), p. 41.

36. Louis R. Harlan, *Booker T. Washington, The Making of a Black Leader* (New York: Oxford University Press, 1972), p. 130.

37. Kirby, *Darkness at the Dawning*, p. 171.

38. Booker T. Washington, "How to Build a Race," Sunday night lecture, *Tuskegee Student* 12 (October 20, 1898), pp. 3–4. Copy in Tuskegee Institute Archives, Tuskegee Institute.

39. August Meier, *Negro Thought in America, 1880-1915* (Ann Arbor, Mich.: University of Michigan Press, 1963), pp. 139–40, 148.

40. Woodward, *Origins of the New South*, pp. 132, 135.

41. Richard A. Straw, "The Collapse of Biracial Unionism: The Alabama Coal Strike of 1908." *Alabama Historical Quarterly* 37 (Summer 1975), p. 93.

42. Booker T. Washington, "The Best Labor in the World," *Southern States Farm Magazine* 5 (January 1898), pp. 496–98. Copy in the Booker T. Washington Papers, Container 864, Library of Congress, Washington, D.C.

43. Richart T. Ely and George S. Wehrwein, *Land Economics* (New York: Macmillan, 1910), p. 205.

44. Work, *Negro Year Book*, pp. 163, 167, 180.

45. Meier and Rudwick, *From Plantation to Ghetto*, p. 233.

46. George Brown Tindall, *The Emergence of the New South* (Baton Rouge, La.: Louisiana State University Press, 1967), p. 33.

47. Clara Eliot, *The Farmer's Campaign for Credit* (New York: Appleton, 1927), p. 156.

48. Arthur M. Ford, *The Political Economics of Rural Poverty in the South* (Cambridge, Mass.: Ballinger Publishing Company, 1973), p. 20; Robert Browne, "Black Land Loss: The Plight of Black Ownership," *Southern Exposure* (Autumn 1974), p. 11.

49. Tindall, *The Emergence of the New South*, pp. 33–34; Eliot, *The Farmer's Campaign for Credit,* pp. 156–60.

50. John Kenneth Galbraith, "The Farm Problem and Policy Choices," in Edmund S. Phelps et al., *Problems of the Modern Economy* (New York: Norton, 1966), p. 151; Arthur S. Link, "The Cotton Crisis, the South and Anglo-American Diplomacy," in J. Carlyle Sitterson, ed., *Studies in Southern History* (Chapel Hill, N.C.: University of North Carolina Press, 1957), pp. 122–38; Theodore Saloutos, *Farmer Movements in the South, 1965–1933* (Berkeley, Calif.: University of California Press, 1960), pp. 238–48.

51. Robert R. Moton to J.F. Duggar, September 13, 1916; Carl Vrodman to Robert R. Moton, October 4, 1916, both letters in the Robert Russa Moton General Correspondence, Container 7, Tuskegee Institute Archives, Tuskegee Institute.

52. Monroe N. Work, *Negro Year Book 1918–19* (Tuskegee: Tuskegee Institute Press, 1919), p. 368.

53. Ransom and Sutch, *One Kind of Freedom,* pp. 172–74.

54. Haystead and Fite, *The Agricultural Regions of the United States,* p. 112.

55. Hanes Walton, Jr., *Black Republicans: The Politics of the Black and Tans* (Metuchen, N.J.: Scarecrow Press, 1975), pp. 81–84.

56. On black politics in Alabama between 1890 and World War I, see Sheldon Hackney, *Populism to Progressivism in Alabama* (Princeton, N.J.: Princeton University Press, 1969) and Mary Tucker, "The Negro in the Populist Movement in Alabama, 1890-1896," master's thesis, Atlanta University, 1957.

57. Work, *Negro Year Book, 1918-19,* p. 374.

58. Carter G. Woodson, *A Century of Negro Migration* (New York: Associated Publishers, 1918), p. 169.

59. Haystead and Fite, *The Agricultural Regions of the United States,* pp. 123, 128.

60. Ibid., p. 116. As late as 1940, only 2.7 percent of all farms in Mississippi owned tractors.

61. Ransom and Sutch, *One Kind of Freedom,* p. 196.

62. Paul M. Sweezy, *The Theory of Capitalist Development* (New York: Monthly Review Press, 1942), pp. 272–73.

chapter 2

THE MOBILE BLACK FAMILY: SOCIOLOGICAL IMPLICATIONS
Frank G. Pogue

MIGRATION

CASE ONE

Mr. and Mrs. X, natives of Orville, Alabama, and former sharecroppers, were parents of eight children—five boys and three girls. Like many black families, they were lucky enough to have had parents who had, through some source, inherited property. Mr. X had inherited and purchased some 80 acres and Mrs. X had inherited 34 acres in rural Alabama. During their marriage they accumulated an additional 15 acres, constructed two homes, and purchased cattle, horses, pigs, and other livestock. Approximately 10 acres were used yearly as farmland and much of the rest housed prized timber.

By most standards, the family was stable and secure. They were "God-fearing," church-going people.

As the family matured something began happening—when the children reached eighteen or twenty years old they moved from the South to several large urban northern and eastern cities. One went to New York City, one to Chicago, three to Cleveland, one to San Francisco, and two to Detroit. All are married and have families of their own.

Mr. X died in 1972, leaving all possessions to his wife. Mrs. X, who was unable to maintain the farm and residual properties, made several unsuccessful attempts to convince her sons to return to Orville. She then tried to attract her daughters. Both efforts failed.

Mrs. X died in 1974, leaving equal shares of the land and its contents to the eight children. Within a short time all 139 acres were sold to a large electrical company. The timber has been cut and trucked away, leaving miles of bare and corrosive land. A large electrical outlet (station) occupies a vast portion. Another large section has been converted into a "Restricted-Posted" area for hunting and fishing for customers/ supporters of the industry.

This land is gone.

CASE TWO

Mr. and Mrs. Y of rural Louisiana were owners of 86 acres of timber land, and parents of six children, all of whom are married with families of their own.

Unlike the children of Mr. and Mrs. X, all of the children of Mr. and Mrs. Y had not moved to urban areas; four of the six had remained.

Following the death of Mrs. Y, and inasmuch as he was approaching eighty, Mr. Y moved from the farm to live with his oldest son. The farm quickly deteriorated. After two years of urban living Mr. Y died, leaving everything to his children. The land (property) was divided equally, with each child receiving approximately 14 acres.

One by one the four children that remained in the rural area sold their land, left their homes, and moved to urban centers. The two children who had already left also sold their land.

The land is presently owned by several small and middle-sized industries that have themselves moved from urban to rural areas. It has been raped of its serenity.

This land is gone.

CASE THREE

Mr. and Mrs. Z of rural South Carolina were parents of eleven children—six girls and five boys. They were pillars of their rural town and local church; the high school was named after the family.

Over a period of twenty years, ten of their children married and moved to large urban areas. Four are divorced. Mr. Z was killed in an automobile accident, leaving more than 80 acres of land to Mrs. Z.

Mrs. Z's youngest son lives and works in Cleveland. She has tried several times to lure him back to the rural South. Since this seems hopeless, she is thinking of selling all of her land and moving to Cleveland, where several of her children live.

This land is not gone but unless Mrs. Z discovers its importance, it will be sold.

Without doubt, these stories and countless others are familiar to many. In fact, thousands of urban dwellers can cite examples that would describe even more vividly black movement to central cities in the North, East, and West (as well as to urban southern cities), and are familiar with the socioeconomic and psychological effects of this migration on the fiber of the black family. Not all who moved owned land, but most could associate personal sweat and hardship with someone else's land. After all, blacks were systematically brought from Africa and rigidly placed into close association with land in the New World.

A report released by McGee and Boone revealed that the South's former slaves amassed an estimated 15 million acres of land in the United States by 1910, and that the figure is now down to 5 million acres.[1] This rate of land exchange suggests that by the year 2000 black rural landownership will be nonexistent.

The fact that physical mobility is itself disruptive has been of concern to many scholars.[2] The migration of blacks northward from the rural South took on the aspect of a mass movement about the year 1914; this became one of the most significant events in the history of black Americans in the twentieth century.[3] The movement was so noticeable that at least one group observed:

They're leaving Memphis in Droves,
Some are coming on the passenger,
Some are coming on the freight,
Others will be found walking,
For none have time to wait.[4]

The years preceding World War I and the period preceding and through World War II saw a mass black exodus of overwhelming proportions from rural to urban centers and from the South to the North and West. A people who in 1900 were 77 percent rural, in half a century became more than 65 percent urban.[5] Although recent mobility trends for 1965 and 1975 show a marked slowdown, it is revealing to note that the South lost only 1 percent of its black population from 1965 to 1975. Presently, 53 percent of the black population is in the South, 39 percent is in the North, 19 percent is in the Northeast, 20 percent is in north central states, and 9 percent is in western states.[6] According to 1974 data, only 8 percent of the black population can be identified as "nonmetropolitan dwellers," a change from 10.3 percent in 1960, and 9.1 percent in 1970.[7]

The declining black farm population in the South and Southeast is accompanied by a continuing heavy migration of black youths to urban centers. Statistics show that there are nearly three times as many youths in the 10-14 age group in the South as there are in the 20-24 age category, and there are considerably more than three times as many aged 15–19 as there are in the 25–29 age group.[8] Assuredly, there are not enough job opportunities on farms to absorb the maturing black youth population. Families cannot be sustained without work.

Where are black families today? Many colleagues and students, primarily black, are astonished when data are presented showing the distribution of the black population in the United States. Most, when asked to identify the top-ranking state where blacks live, invariably name a southern city—Atlanta, Georgia, is most often mentioned. The

TABLE 2.1   **Distribution of Black Population in the United States for Selected States, January 1, 1977**

State	Black Population	State	Black Population
New York	2,960,375	Pennsylvania	1,169,990
California	1,811,589	North Carolina	1,111,187
Illinois	1,755,662	Louisiana	1,097,644
Texas	1,533,695	Ohio	1,079,399
Michigan	1,259,234	New Jersey	1,000,463
Florida	1,197,505	Alabama	823,006
Georgia	1,191,673	South Carolina	754,081

Source: Official 1970 Census of Population, prepared by SRDS Consumer Market Data Division (January 1, 1977).

reality is, as table 2.1 shows, that New York State is home for about 3 million black Americans, and has the largest state concentration of blacks in the United States. New York is followed by California, with almost two million blacks; Illinois, with 1.7 million; Texas, with 1.5 million; and Michigan, with 1.2 million. It is revealing to note that for the twelve states with one million or more blacks, only five are located in the South or Southwest; six states could be classified as "northern" or "northeastern"; only one, California, can be classified as "far west." The black population remains a northeastern phenomenon.

Further analysis of the distribution of black population according to major cities reveals that New York City ranks number one among cities where blacks are found. In fact, nearly 2.5 million blacks are considered residents of New York City. Although Atlanta, Georgia, is most frequently thought of as the single city where blacks are in the greatest abundance, it is clear that New York City has the greatest number of blacks, followed by Chicago, Los Angeles, Philadelphia, Detroit, and Washington, D.C. In fact, the eight top-ranking cities with the highest concentration of blacks are not "southern" in nature.

TABLE 2.2 **Distribution of Black Population in the United States for 16 Cities, January 1, 1977**

City	Black Population	City	· Black Population
New York	2,470,906	Houston	477,631
Chicago	1,520,134	St. Louis	423,521
Los Angeles-LB	1,000,677	San Francisco-Oakland	414,240
Philadelphia	999,902	Atlanta	392,201
Detroit	962,800	Cleveland	378,208
Washington, D.C.	878,808	Dallas-Fort Worth	312,233
Baltimore	564,884	New Orleans	369,480
Newark, N.J.	482,203	Memphis	314,963

Source: Official 1970 Census of Population, prepared by SRDS Consumer Market Data Division (January 1, 1977).

It is comforting to note that after three decades of a predominately one-way migration stream from the South to the North and West, a new pattern of black migration appears to be emerging in the 1970s. There is some evidence that during the four-year period from 1970 to 1974, the volume of black outmigration *from* the South declined and, at the same time, the number moving *to* the South increased. In fact, during this four-year period the number of blacks four years old and over *moving to* the South closely approximated the number moving *from* the South—276,000 immigrants versus 241,000 outmigrants.[9]

Although this reverse migration has not revealed significant moves to the rural South, especially to rural farms, it does mean that a larger number of blacks are realizing that there have been significant changes in the South which provide greater opportunities than before slavery, Jim Crow, and the lynching periods. That this reverse migration has caught the imagination of some was illustrated in a "made-for-television" portrayal of a black family returning to the South. Tyson, Hooks, and their children revealed the ingrained fears of what this "return to southern roots" means for a large segment of black urban dwellers.

Reverse migration, however, shows that this tendency to return to the South is directly related to socioeconomic factors. Average low-income black families are not yet returning; rather, they account for more than 74 percent of the blacks who migrated North or West during the period 1970– 1974. More than 65 percent of the 276,000 blacks who did return were educated (some college training, a bachelor's degree, some graduate training, or a graduate degree) or skilled. They returned to enter professional careers, politics and business. While they have not purchased large quantities of rural farmland they do purchase homes or residual properties. Clearly, the socio-political and racist factors that gave rise to black migration have not changed significantly for low-income, uneducated, or unskilled black families.

How can this situation for low-income southern blacks be reversed and how can urban blacks recognize increasing signs of institutional racism? One obvious strategy must be to continue to destroy the myths associated with physical mobility and success. Hopefully, such observations and demonstrations will identify these ill-founded beliefs and cause the average black family to reassess the promise of "greater opportunities in the North, East and West."

What migrating black families found at the end of the rainbow was not "gold." What they learned was that to be black in Mississippi, Georgia, Alabama, or Tennessee, was to be black in New York, Chicago, Detroit, or San Francisco. The key is blackness. Geography makes little difference.

Denied a decent livelihood and recourse to the law, the black family was further intimidated by the near impunity allowed lynch mobs. Their main defense and protest against lynching, against the wage differentials, and against the many frustrations of life was to move North.[10]

What was true then, remains true today; the North is "no land of milk and honey with dollars growing on trees."[11]

EMPLOYMENT AND EDUCATION

Black families have been faced with unemployment and underemployment as well as systematic exclusion from the employment process. Blacks, even during periods of relative national prosperity, have historically suffered a disproportionate share of joblessness. While there is just reason for alarm at the high unemployment rate for the nation during this decade, black joblessness has averaged over 8 percent between 1970 and 1976 (See table 2.3).

TABLE 2.3   **Black Unemployment in the United States, 1970–1976 (annual percentages: national)**

Year	Black	White
1970	8.2	4.5
1971	9.9	5.4
1972	10.0	5.0
1973	8.9	4.3
1974	9.9	5.0
1975	10.9	6.8
1976	14.3	7.5

Source: U.S. Department of Labor, Bureau of Labor Statistics.

In 1975 and 1976, black unemployment for some specific areas was generally over 14 percent and as high as 50 percent in many low-income communities. If current trends continue, a large segment of our black youth—about half—will be unemployed over the next five years and will constitute a permanent "workless" class.

In 1970, there were more than 4 million persons unemployed in the United States. This represents 4.9 percent of the total employable population. Of the total number unemployed, 752,000 were black. This was a ratio of 8.2 percent for the black population.[12]

In April 1976, the ratio of unemployment for all workers was 5.7 percent. It was 5.4 percent for white workers and 9.9 percent for blacks, a differential deficit ratio of 77 percent for black Americans as compared to white Americans.

Correlated closely with the high rate of unemployment was the distribution of those annually employed by types of occupations (underemployment). In June 1967, 45.5 percent of all blacks employed as compared with 15.1 percent of whites were occupied in the lower-paying jobs, such as private household workers, service workers, and laborers, and only 10.2 percent of blacks were employed as professionals, managers, or proprietors as compared to 28.4 percent of the white population.[13]

Despite proclamations by the Ford administration that the recession was ending, 20 million workers experienced unemployment during the course of 1976. And thirty years after the enactment of the 1946 Employment Act, the government's commitment to full employment was still at the discussion stage—perhaps because this was an election year in which administrative officials could engage in an insensitive debate about "acceptable levels" of unemployment and cite joblessness rates (7.5 percent for whites and 14 percent for blacks) as "tolerable."

Black families are also negatively affected by income disparities, especially during a period of inflation. In 1973, the median income for white families was $12,345, while for the black family it was $8,815 or a deficit of $3,530.[14] Blacks have the lowest income of all minority groups in the United States.

It should also be observed that in 1973, 70 percent of all white families had an income level of $8,000 and above per year as compared to 42 percent of black families. Nearly 50 percent of all white families were in the income category of $10,000 and above as compared to 22 percent of black families, and 21 percent of all white families were in the $15,000 and above category as compared to 7.2 percent of black families.[15]

The geographic interruption of family life was also justified by associating such moves with greater access to educational opportunities. Black families, interested in educational and occupational mobility for their children, moved swiftly to seek similar advantages that had become realities for the typical white urban American, including more recent ethnic arrivals. The "separate but equal" educational system, the Law of the South, coupled with constant external negative influences, did little to encourage immobility and stability.

Black families learned early that one of the most effective ways to crystalize and legitimize segregation and discrimination was to deny access to quality education. Such denial leads to an inability to perform normatively in competitive situations. That this was true is revealed in Ashmore's 1952 study, *The Negro and the Schools*. Ashmore found noticeable discrepancies between the amount of money spent for the education of black and white children in southern states. The average was $164.83 for the education of one white pupil, as compared with $115.08, or 70 percent of that amount, for the education of each black child.[16] The amount of money spent per black pupil varied anywhere from 30 percent of what was spent per white pupil in Mississippi to 85 percent in North Carolina. In the same year the capital outlay per pupil for black schools in southern states was $29.58, or 82 percent of the $36.25 spent per white pupil.[17] The simple fact is that racism was so pronounced, blacks were systematically denied equal access to educational self-enhancement, producing negative self-images for millions of black children. Such negative images were reinforced by high black absenteeism from school, poor teaching, and inadequate library holdings.

Even the most casual observer can note that the dream of educational enhancement is not yet realized. Instead of the anticipated inclusion, blacks are still systematically excluded from the educational process. Mobility and its positive consequences work slower for blacks.

After struggling for years to demand decent public education, blacks have found that "public education" in this country is in serious trouble, particularly in the central cities. In a speech to the South Carolina Education Association in Columbia, James A. Harris, then president of the National Education Association, painted a threatening picture with these facts:

1. There are nearly two million school-aged children who are not enrolled in school. Most live in large cities.
2. Of the students who are attending classes, more of them will spend some portion of their lives in correctional institutions of higher learning.
3. On any given school day, you will find 13,000 kids of school age in correctional institutions and another 100,000 in jail or police lockups.
4. Of every 100 students attending school across the nation, 23 drop out, 77 graduate from high school, 43 enter college, 21 receive a B.A., six earn an M.A., and one earns a Ph.D.
5. Crime and violence in central city schools are growing at unprecedented rates.
6. Many states now spend more money to incarcerate a child than to provide him with an education. In Iowa, for example, the state

will pay $9,000 a year to maintain a student in a juvenile home, but only $1,050 a year for an ordinary student.[18]
These findings are significantly worse for blacks.

In short, then, black families are finding that schooling (public schooling) in the large metropolitan areas where they terminated migration is not working. In fact, it is failing miserably. Instead of black inclusion, blacks are overwhelmingly excluded from the educational process. These observations can be considered factors giving rise to the slowdown of migration from the rural-urban South.

HOMEOWNERSHIP

Black families have also discovered that the probability of owning their own home is less likely in large urban centers. In 1973, about 7 million housing units were occupied by black households and approximately 62.4 million by white households. About 43 percent of black households lived in homes they owned or were buying, a smaller proportion than the comparable figure of 67 percent of white households.[19]

Owner occupancy rates for black households tended to vary by region. For blacks in the Northeast, only about three out of ten households were buying or owned their home; in the South, the comparable proportion was about five out of ten.[20]

This is, in large measure, due to the increased cost of housing in the urban and northern communities, accompanied by a greater demand for adequacy. It does not, as Billingsly so aptly notes, suggest that southern black families are better housed than their northern counterparts, although it may suggest a greater investment and a sense of belonging on the part of southern home-owning black families.[21]

MEDICAL HEALTH CARE

Although they need so much more medical/health care than whites, black families, as the late Whitney Young observed, get so much less.[22] This is illustrated by records of medical and dental visits for 1973.[23] Blacks were less likely than whites to have visited a physician or dentist: 70 percent of the black population made at least one visit to a physician; only one-third made a visit to a dentist. Furthermore, black persons with lower family incomes were less likely to have received more care in a clinic than blacks with higher family income.[24]

It is also significant to note that life expectancy for blacks continued to be lower than for whites. Among blacks, the average life expectancy at birth in 1973 was 61.9 years for males and 70.1 for females; corresponding figures for whites were 68.4 and 76.1.[25]

FAMILY STRUCTURE

Mobile black families show greater signs of marital instability than those who do not migrate. While this is true it should in no way be interpreted negatively. The black family is stable; approximately 61 percent of the estimated 5.5 million black families in 1975 had both spouses present.[26]

Although the black family is stable it should be observed that the proportion of black families headed by a woman (with no spouse present) climbed from 28 percent in 1970 to 35 percent in 1975 and seems to be leveling off.[27]

From the beginning of the decade to 1974, the number of black women who were heads of their own families increased by .5 million, or 37 percent.[28] Some explanations given include: (1) increasing divorce and separation rates; (2) the retention of children by unwed mothers with greater economic independence; and (3) the availability of public assistance. To this list must be added the existence of employment discrimination directed at black men and women—especially black men—that results in their inability to support their families.

These and other conditions force one to ask how the black family has survived. It is quite clear that the educational, political, economic, and criminal justice systems have failed (and are still failing) to meet the needs of the black family.

Neither geographical nor social mobility has successfully interfered with the black family's informal or formal relationships and ties. Regardless of movements, their family networks have not been disrupted. For proof of this, all one has to do is observe automobile and air traffic. The cars and planes bringing blacks from Detroit, Cleveland, Chicago, and points North, and from Los Angeles, San Francisco, and points West all represent continued and lasting family stability.

One should also note that fewer and fewer relatives are returning North, East, and West with these occasional seasonal visitors. Instead, larger numbers are remaining in rural nonfarm areas.

CONCLUSION

Landownership, therefore, becomes important because it provides an economic base for sociopsychological release and/or identification even for blacks who have migrated. Land serves as an economic and psychological link for the many blacks who are locked behind jail and prison walls; for those who, because of their blackness, are daily brutalized by police; for those who are victims of drugs and alcohol; for those who are consistently denied access to adequate quality health care services; for those who are overrepresented among the unemployed and underemployed; for those who are denied equal access to educational opportunities; and for those who are forced to live in rat-infested houses and substandard housing.

Ownership of land in a capitalistic society implies permanence and political power. The land itself is permanent—something that can be passed on from one generation to the next, representing economic stability for black families.

While the legal and political aspects of landownership must be of central concern, it is also important to present those institutional failures that have been allowed to exist which may often account for the misconceptions blacks have of the promises of mobility.

NOTES

1. Leo McGee and Robert Boone, "Black Rural Land Ownership: A Matter of Economic Survival" (Nashville: Tennessee University Press, 1976), p. 1.

2. See, for example, W.E.B. Du Bois, *The Philadelphia Negro* (New York: Blom, 1967), pp. 25–45; E. Franklin Frazer, *The Negro in the United States,* rev. ed. (New York: Macmillan, 1957), pp. 229–69; Gunnar Myrdal, *The American Dilemma* (New York: Harper, 1963), pp. 157–201; Gilbert Osofsky, *Harlem: The Making of a Ghetto, Negro New York, 1890-1930* (New York: Harper and Row, 1966), pp. 3–178.

3. Dewey H. Palmer, "Moving North: Migration of Negroes During World War I," *Phylon* 28, no. 1 (1967), pp. 52–62.

4. Chicago Commission on Race Relations, "The Negro in Chicago: A Study of Race Relations and a Race Riot" (Chicago: Aldine Publishing Company, 1922), p. 89.

5. James H. Hubert, "Urbanization and the Negro," National Conference of Social Work, Proceedings, 1933 (New York; Macmillan, 1934), p. 41.

6. U.S., Department of Commerce, Bureau of the Census, "Social and Economic Status of the Black Population in the United States" (Washington, D.C.: U.S. Government Printing Office, 1974), p. 13.

7. Ibid., p. 15.

8. These findings were revealed as early as 1963 and continue through 1974. See Selz C. Mayo and C. Horace, "The Rural Negro Population of the South in Transition," *Phylon* 24, no. 2 (1963), pp. 160–71.

9. Bureau of the Census, "Social and Economic Status of the Black Population," pp. 1–10.

10. New Orleans *Time-Picayune,* January 2, 1976, p. 6.

11. Palmer, "Moving North," p. 56.

12. U.S., Department of Commerce, Bureau of the Census, *Statistical Abstracts of the United States* (Washington, D.C.: U.S. Government Printing Office, 1971), p. 215.

13. U.S., Department of Health, Education and Welfare, P. H. S., National Center for Health Statistics, *Differentials in Health Characteristics by Color, United States, July, 1965–June, 1967* (Washington, D.C.: U.S. Government Printing Office, 1969), p. 3.

14. Bureau of the Census, *Statistical Abstracts,* 1974, p. 137.

15. Ibid.

16. Harry S. Ashmore, *The Negro and the Schools* (Chapel Hill, N.C.: University of North Carolina Press, 1954), p. 153.

17. Ibid., p. 156.

18. James A. Harris, "Educational Issues; Implications for Major Cities," Annual Conference, South Carolina Education Association, Columbia, S.C., April 25, 1974, pp. 2 16.

19. Ashmore, *Negroes and the Schools,* p. 134.

20. Ibid. See also U.S., Department of Commerce, "Social and Economic Status of Negroes in the United States" (Washington, D.C.: U.S. Government Printing Office, 1970), pp. 441 42; Andrew Billingsley, *Black Families in White America* (Englewood Cliffs, N.J.: Prentice-Hall, 1968), pp. 93–99, 184–85; Karl E. Taeuber and Alma F. Taeuber, *Negroes in Cities* (Chicago: Aldine Publishing Company, 1965), p. 36.

21. Billingsley, *Black Families,* p. 90.

22. Whitney Young, *Health Care and the Negro Population* (New York: National Urban League, 1964), p. 4.

23. Bureau of the Census, *Statistical Abstracts,* 1971, p. 127.

24. Ibid.

25. Ibid., p. 122.

26. Bureau of the Census, "Social and Economic Status of the Black Population," p. 106.

27. Ibid.

28. U.S., Department of Commerce, Bureau of the Census, "Female Family Heads," Current Population Report, Series P-23, no. 51 (Washington, D.C.: Social and Economic Statistics Administration, 1975), pp. 1–2.

chapter 3

OWNERSHIP AND CONTROL OF RESOURCES BY MINORITIES AND SMALL FARMERS IN THE SOUTH

James A. Lewis

INTRODUCTION

Equity or justice is a concept heavily laden with individual values. Economists, conscious of scientific paradigms, tend to concentrate on issues of efficiency and physical allocation because they are quantifiable; we often conveniently leave value judgments to the politician, sociologist, voter, or hopefully, the reader. An initial step in this analysis is to recognize the interrelationship between equity and efficiency. Samuels says that:

> ... the problem of social efficiency is how to maintain "equitable" income distribution, power structure, and other arrangements and still have efficiency in the sense of prices equal to marginal costs, a statement which is a purely positive proposition. Equity is very much mixed up with efficiency; or, to say the same thing in other words, institutional arrangements figure very much in economic efficiency.[1]

Once the quantifiable efficiency criteria are satisfied the stumbling block of value, equity, or justice can be addressed. A way of arriving at these concerns is to look at the equality of ownership and control of power. The item of concern becomes who are the "haves" and the "have nots," and "how much" does each group hold? Boulding inquires, for example:

> ... What is the optimum degree of inequality or equality in a society? This is a question from which conventional economics recoils in horror as being completely beyond its capability. It is

1. A small number of black farmers have been able to purchase modern equipment and make their farms into a profitable business. *Photo by John Cross*

surely a question, however, which in regard to economic good or economic welfare is in the province of the economist, even though he might be disposed to leave the question of ultimate spiritual equality to the philosopher or theologian. If economists, however, cannot apply their tools and skills to the examination of the problem of economic equality who can substitute for them?

Economic equality can be measured, at least roughly, in terms of a number of possible properties of the distribution either of income or of wealth among individuals. Having half a dozen possible measures does not detract from the fact that this many, even when inconsistent, are better than none. Most of the measures do move in the same direction . . . .[2]

A study of the relative resource holdings of different groups of farm-owners and operators provides insight in terms of equality. Equity considerations in the framework of how much each group should have are matters of judgment, and it is difficult if not impossible to find universal consensus.

Rather than attack the problem from a subjective analysis of equity, this chapter compares and contrasts farm operators in the southern states with respect to race, number of operators, and ownership and control of land, capital, and farm product sales. Factual data will help to identify some equity issues concerning farm operators.

AN AGGREGATE OVERVIEW

Resources in a neoclassical economic framework can be evaluated in terms of land, labor, and capital. *Land* has attributes of wealth, status in the community, equality, security, power, and piety.[3] *Labor* represents the human input into the system. Finally, *capital* refers to the instruments that are made to produce other goods. The measures presented here as indicators of these resources are, respectively:[4] land—land in farms and land owned; labor—number of operators and number of landowners reported in the 1969 Census of Agriculture; and capital— value of land and buildings, and estimated market value of machinery and equipment reported by respondents to the census questionnaire.[5] Granted, these are crude measures of total resources owned and controlled by southern farm operators, but the emphasis is on relative dis-

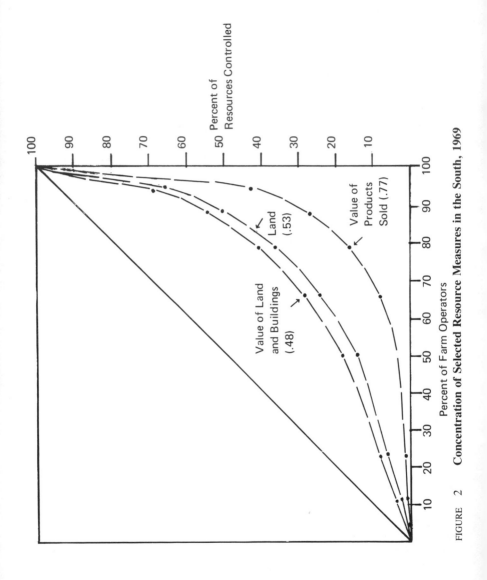

FIGURE 2   Concentration of Selected Resource Measures in the South, 1969

tributions. The proxy for earnings, wealth, or economic power in agriculture is value of products sold (that is, the economic class of farm).

Table 3.1 shows the distribution of selected measures of resource ownership and control by economic class in the southern states.[6] At one end of the scale are the Class 6, part-time, part-retirement farms, with less than $2,500 gross annual sales. These smaller farms represented 49 percent of all farm operators in the South in 1969, but they accounted for less than 4 percent of gross farm sales. They controlled 15 percent of the land in farms, 20 percent of the land owned by farm operators, 18 percent of the value of land and buildings, and 19 percent of the market value of machinery and equipment.

At the opposite end of the scale were the Class 1 farms, reporting over $40,000 gross annual sales. These larger farms represented 5 percent of all farms in the South but accounted for 55 percent of gross farm sales. They controlled 32 percent of land in farms, 27 percent of land owned by farm operators, 29 percent of the value of land and buildings, and 26 percent of the market value of machinery and equipment.[7]

One way of comparing equality of ownership and control is the concentration curve. Some examples for land, capital, and economic power are plotted in Figure 2. The curves are discontinuous because they represent cumulative percentages of holdings at each economic class category and are actually point estimates. Enough data are available, however, to sketch the expected appearance of concentration curves for these resource measures relative to the number of farm operators. Estimated Gini ratios appear in parentheses under each respective resource measure. These ratios reflect the relative degrees of concentration of control. Capital, with a Gini ratio of .48 for the value of land and buildings, is slightly less concentrated than land in farms with a Gini ratio of .54.

Economic importance, as measured by value of products sold, is considerably more concentrated than either land in farms of value of land and buildings shown by a Gini ratio of .77. This concentration implies that power in terms of economic importance (sales) is relatively more concentrated in the hands of a few operators than the other measures. The farther the curves extend from the 45° diagonal, the more concentrated is ownership or control of the item being measured. If equality is the objective, we would prefer lower Gini ratios, and concentration curves which more closely approach the diagonal.

TABLE 3.1 **Selected Measures of and Percent Distribution of Resource Ownership and Control by Economic Class* for Farm Operators, Southern States, 1969**

									Noncommercial farms	
									Part-time	Part-retirement
Item	Unit	All farms	Class 1	Class 2	Class 3	Class 4	Class 5	Class 6		
		Number	*Percent*							
Value of products sold	mil. dol.	12,779	55.6	16.1	11.1	7.9	4.9	.1	2.1	.1
Number of farm operators	numbers	1,117,336	5.4	6.6	8.9	13.2	16.5	11.0	26.7	11.9
Number of landowners	numbers	989,517	5.4	6.3	8.4	12.2	16.2	11.1	27.5	12.8
Land in farms**	1,000 acres	324,989	32.6	15.1	13.8	12.1	10.8	3.3	8.1	3.8
Land owned**	1,000 acres	229,536	27.9	13.1	12.7	12.7	12.7	4.5	10.3	5.7
Value of land and buildings	mil. dol.	66,943	29.3	14.6	13.5	12.1	11.5	3.8	10.4	4.2
Value of machinery and equipment	mil. dol.	7,355	26.3	15.4	13.9	12.6	11.8	4.4	11.3	3.9

*Definitions of economic class of farms, in annual farm product sales:

Class 1—$40,000 or more
Class 2—$20,000–$39,999
Class 3—$10,000–$19,999
Class 4—$ 5,000–$ 9,999
Class 5—$ 2,500–$ 4,999
Class 6—$50–$2,499 farm product sales, and an operator under 65 years who worked off the farm less than 100 days
Part-time—$50–$2,499 farm product sales, and an operator under 65 years who worked off the farm more than 100 days
Part-retirement—$50–$2,499 farm product sales, and an operator 65 years or older

**Number of farm operators who reported and owned and the acreage of land owned.

Source: U. S. Bureau of Census, Census of Agriculture, 1969, vol. 1, Area Reports, pt. 26, sect. 1, Summary Data, U.S. Government Printing Office, Washington, D.C., 1972.

MINORITIES AND SMALL FARM OPERATORS

There are slightly more than 89,000 minority farm operators[8]; they represent 7.9 percent of all farm operators in the South (see table 1.2). Average annual sales per farm for white operators was just over $12,000. For minorities it was almost $3,400. This indicates that the median economic class for white operators is Class 3, and for minority farmers it is Class 5. Almost 85 percent of minority farm operators sold less than $5,000 value in farm products and 94 percent sold less than $10,000. Although white operators were more numerous in the lower sales groups, relatively more of their population fell in Class 1 through Class 4. Table 3.2 shows, for the most part, the relatively unequal distribution of operations by race, as grouped into sales categories. Far less than 1 percent of minorities operated Class 1 farms, compared to about 6 percent of white operators. On the other hand, about 48 percent of white-operated farms and 70 percent of minority-operated farms were classified as Class 6, part-time, and part-retirement units.

Information on the distribution of the other measures of resource ownership and control is limited. However, it is possible to compare operators of Class 1-5 farms and Class 6, part-time, part-retirement operators by race. Table 3.3 shows in more detail the distribution of ownership and control over selected resources for white and minority farm operators in relation to their respective total population groups in the South.

For convenience, the group with less than $2,500 in value of products sold is referred to as "small farms"[9] (Class 6, part-time, and part-retirement categories). These small farms represented more than 70 percent of all minority farm operators and landowners but less than 50 percent of white farm operators and landowners in the South. Minority operators of small farms differ from their white counterparts in terms of the value of products sold. Over 16 percent of all products sold by minorities were from the small-farm operators. Less than 4 percent of all products sold by whites were from small-farm operators. A significant number of white and minority operators can be classified as small farmers. More than a fourth of the small farmers were part-time operators; they accounted for the largest share of small-farm contributions to the value of products sold.

White small-farm operators controlled 14 percent of all land in farms

TABLE 3.2 **Number of Farm Operators and Percent Distribution by Economic Class* and Race, Southern States, 1969**

Item	All Farms	Class 1	Class 2	Class 3	Class 4	Class 5	Noncommercial farms		
							Class 6	Part-time	Part-retirement
	Number	*Percent*							
White operators	1,029,081	5.8	7.0	9.4	12.2	16.7	10.1	26.7	11.0
Minority operators	89,285	0.1	1.4	4.0	9.1	14.4	21.9	26.6	21.7

*Definitions of economic class of farms, in annual farm product sales:

    Class 1—$40,000 or more
    Class 2—$20,000–$39,999
    Class 3—$10,000–$19,999
    Class 4—$ 5,000–$ 9,999
    Class 5—$ 2,500–$ 4,999
    Class 6—$50–$2,499 farm product sales, and an operator under 65 years who worked off the farm less than 100 days
    Part-time—$50–$2,499 farm product sales, and an operator under 65 years who worked off the farm more than 100 days
    Part-retirement—$50–$2,499 farm product sales, and an operator 65 years or older

Source: U.S. Bureau of Census, Census of Agriculture, 1969, vol. 1, Area Reports. pt. 26, sect. 1, Summary Data, U.S. Government Printing Office, Washington, D.C., 1972.

TABLE 3.3 **Distribution of Farm Resource Ownership and Control by Race and Economic Class, Southern States, 1969***

Item	Unit	All farms		Class 1-5 farms		All noncommercial farms		Class 6 farms		Noncommercial farms			
										Part-time farms		Part-retirement farms	
		White	Minority	White	Minority	White	Minority	White	Minority	White	Minority	White	Minority
		Number					*Percent*						
Value of products sold	mil. dol.	12,477	302	95.9	83.2	3.7	16.1	.8	5.4	2.0	6.2	.1	4.0
Number of farm operators	numbers	1,028,081	89,285	52.1	29.7	47.9	70.3	10.1	21.9	26.7	26.7	11.0	21.7
Number of land operators	numbers	917,974	71,543	50.2	26.7	49.7	73.3	10.3	21.4	27.5	27.3	11.9	24.1
Land in farms	1,000 acres	317,122	7,868	85.2	55.1	14.5	43.6	3.0	12.5	7.9	16.9	3.6	14.6
Land owned	1,000 acres	223,458	6,078	79.9	47.2	19.7	50.9	4.2	14.7	10.1	18.4	5.4	18.2
Value of land and buildings	mil. dol.	64,816	2,126	81.9	51.9	17.5	46.3	3.5	13.6	10.1	18.5	3.9	14.2
Value of machinery and equipment	mil. dol.	7,046	308	81.2	54.1	18.5	45.7	3.9	14.3	10.9	19.6	3.6	11.8

Source: See source, table 1.1.

*Defined in note of table 1.1. Percentages are computed for whites in each economic class as percent of all whites, and for minorities in each economic class as percent of all minorities.

and owned almost 20 percent of all white-owned land in the South in 1969. Minority small-farm operators controlled about 44 percent of all minority-operated land in farms and owned over 50 percent of all minority-owned land.[10] Within the small-farm group, part-time operators controlled the most land regardless of race; this amounted to 43.9 million and 3.1 million acres, respectively. Minority farm operators held less in absolute terms, regardless of the resource measure used.

The majority of capital assets in the form of land, buildings, machinery, and equipment values was held by Class 1-5 operators, regardless of race. However, minority small farmers controlled close to 46 percent of minority capital assets, while white small farmers held only 18 percent of white capital assets. Again, part-time operators were the most significant asset holders within the small-farm group, regardless of race.

With regard to economic importance, land, labor, or capital resources, there was an unequal distribution of ownership and control across the range of southern farm operators grouped by annual sales categories. The inequality of these resource ownership and control measures is intensified when race is taken into consideration. Minority small farmers made up a greater share of the minority farming population in terms of sales or resource ownership and control than did their white counterparts. However, even though white small farmers represented only 4 percent of total sales, they accounted for almost half of all white operators, and controlled almost one-fifth of white-controlled land and capital assets. From the perspective of owners and controllers of basic rural resources, these people, whether white or minority, are an important group of private decision-makers who merit more attention in the future. Bawden says that we should "... direct a portion of our energy and resources to the problems of *all* rural residents at the expense of the attention we now devote to the commercial farmer."[11]

Title V of the Rural Development Act is aimed at stimulating research and extension activities on small farms. However, of the initial $45 million authorized under this act, less than 1 percent has been appropriated.[12] Full funding of Title V would induce more research and consultative services for the small farmer. This effort would not reach all of the rural residents Bawden suggested, but would at least serve the needs of a portion of that population.

Small farmers have not been completely neglected, however. Recent efforts have been made to evaluate their status and analyze alternative income-earning opportunities.[13] There are several problems, however. To begin with, there is no consistent, clear, or concise definition of a small farm, so the comparability of different studies is limited. It has been suggested that small-farm definitions be expanded to include those with up to $20,000 gross annual sales. Conditions and operating practices of small farmers differ by location, size and type of farm, economic class, objectives, and race. Regardless of definitions, however, few studies address the small farmers identified in this study. Here, small farms are characterized as those with under $2,500 value of products sold; it is a very restricted definition. Since this group owns and controls almost one-fifth of the farm resources, they should warrant greater attention in research, extension, policy, and planning activities. Analysis concerned with resource use and allocation is incomplete if it neglects to account for all decision-making owners and controllers. Differences between economic classes and race indicate the need to distinguish these factors, as well as many others such as age, education, attitudes, type of farm and location, and so on, inferring about resource use, allocation, and policies intended to influence decision-makers.

CONCLUSION

There is an unequal distribution of resources across economic classes of farms, and the inequality is greater when race is taken into consideration. Small farmers own and control a significant amount of land, labor, and capital resources; yet they account for only a small portion of the total value of agricultural products sold. The relevant issues here may or may not be productivity in agriculture; much of the research on small farmers is just beginning to surface. Perhaps the most important points stressed revolve around a needed concern for people who are rural residents and decision-makers, rather than farm producers. Efforts to improve our food and fiber production capability are important but they should not be the unilateral agenda item.

Recent evidence shows that the rate of population growth for nonmetropolitan areas actually exceeds that for metropolitan areas.[14] However, areas with predominantly black populations still have a net outmigration. The overall United States population growth indicates that demands and pressures on rural resources will increase in the future, particularly the demand for land. In addition, the rural population is much broader than a principally agricultural-based community. Disregard of all rural residents, their resource ownership and control, their wealth base, and their status and development in general has a high social cost. As one who is particularly concerned with transitional pressures upon minorities, Browne recently stated that it is:

> . . . cause for somber reflection, for in retrospect it may well prove to have prefigured the decline in the black community's stake in the American nation. . . . In an economy where agriculture contributes less and less to the national income and to the level of employment, the economic significance of this shattering decline in black landownership may not be great. Its social and political significance, however, may be explosive.[15]

The concern about minorities as a specific interest group is well founded, as evidenced by racial disparities identified in this chapter. Many of the problems confronted by minorities may be synonymous with those of small farmers and poor rural residents in general, but this proposition is not supported by racial distinctions identified within the small-farm group. We know very little about small farmers relative to our knowledge of the commercial farming sector.

The information available is limited in coverage. Consequently, the first step in research will be to identify all rural resource owners. Limiting analysis to agriculture, and within that to commercial farms, will ill serve the rural population and will diminish the reliability of any research undertaken.

Increasing research and extension activities for small farmers would change both equity and efficiency relationships. Relative changes between large and small farmers' levels of well-being would occur if the small farmers' status can be improved without making large farmers appreciably worse off. The first step is to determine whether or not small farmers can improve their level of well-being and, if not, to identify the reasons why. Is it explained by resource constraints in the form of market structure, marketing, transportation, taxation, and product-processing disadvantages? Research on small farmers is an initial step in answering the basic questions. Information is an essential ingredient to knowledge, understanding, and problem-solving ability. Before questions can be answered, information needs to be assembled and analyzed.

Research into the problems, status, and perspectives of small farmers should be expanded. Agricultural operations differ by region, type of farm, size of farm, economic class, and race. Analysis which takes these items into consideration, and which includes all farm operators, would be useful. One hypothesis would be that objectives differ by type, economic class, and race of farm operator. Although race would theoretically be a neutral factor, it apparently does make a difference. Our methodology may be too restrictive. In the past, analysis has depended on optimization objectives for the farm operation. Perhaps household objectives conflict with this assumption, since many operators farm for personal satisfaction and rewards to quality of life for themselves and their families. Goals of different operators have as much or greater impact on solutions to optimization problems as do resource constraints. If family income, wealth, welfare, and life-style objectives differ from farm-production objectives, the behavior, responsiveness, and resource allocation of these people would vary from that expected of profit maximizers, loss minimizers, or risk averters.

Preferably, rural residents and resource owners will be included in future research as Bawden has suggested. These people have not necessarily been included in the past. Their control over rural resources is significant and their decisions about resource allocation would have some influence on the effectiveness of public policies concerning resource use.

This chapter has concentrated on a portion of the rural population that is seldom addressed—minorities and small farmers. Efforts to identify, analyze, and provide information about this group of decision-makers is at least one approach to more comprehensive accounting for those who own and control rural resources. The other group—nonfarm resource owners—are yet to be identified and analyzed in terms of their influence and control in the rural economy.

NOTES

1. Warren J. Samuels, "Welfare Economics, Power, and Property," in *Perspectives of Property,* Gene Wunderlich and W. L. Gibson, Jr., ed. (University Park: Institute for Research on Land and Water Resources, Pennsylvania State University, 1972), p. 90.

2. Kenneth E. Boulding, "Econ is a Four Letter Word," *Increasing Un-*

derstanding of Public Problems and Policies (Chicago: Farm Foundation, 1973), p. 142.

3. D. David Moyer et al, *Land Tenure in the United States: Development and Status,* U.S. Dept. of Agriculture, Agricultural Information Bulletin no. 338, June 1969.

4. Unpublished 1969 Census of Agriculture tabulations for minority farm operators for each of the southern states were obtained from the Bureau of the Census. These tabulations classified minorities as nonwhites. Detailed breakdown by racial groups is not possible. These people will hereafter be referred to as minorities. Format of the tabulations was in the form of State Table 9: *Summary of Selected Economic Class Groups,* vol. 1, sec. 1.

5. Admittedly, this variable also includes a significant component of the land resource; however, it was not possible to delineate which portion of the figure was for land. The capital category is not precise in physical terms but incorporates measures of value in dollar terms.

6. Definitions of economic class and the southern states are in table 3.1 notes.

7. At the national level, the last count of U.S. farm operators showed just over 2.7 million farmers. This 1969 Census of Agriculture reported a total of $45.6 billion in farm product sales; 55.6 percent was sold by 8.1 percent of operators having gross annual sales of $40,000 and over. These operators controlled just over a third of land in farms. In contrast, over a third of all operators had less than $2,500 in sales, representing under 2.4 percent of total farm products sold. These operators controlled 13.6 percent of land in farms, 13.1 percent of value of land and buildings, and 11.9 percent of estimated market value of machinery and equipment.

8. Minorities include blacks, Cubans, Mexican-Americans, Japanese, and American Indians; 94 percent of all minorities in the South are blacks.

9. Small farm does not necessarily mean low income; neither is value of products sold a good indicator of economic status. Many persons who operate these farms have supplemental, off-farm family income, or they sell surplus farm production over that needed for home consumption. Their objectives with regard to family income, wealth, welfare, and life style may differ from or alter their farm-production objectives.

10. There are two interesting sidelights with regard to information on land ownership and control. First, land in farms in the South represented only 61 percent of the total land area. Anderson et al. have stated that 1.5 percent of land area in urban uses ("Perspectives on Agricultural Land Policy," *Journal of Soil and Water Conservation,* vol. 30, no. 1, January - February, 1975, p. 36). Combined state and federal land comprised less than 10 percent of the land area. Therefore, almost 28 percent of rural land in the South has not been identified in

the context of ownership and control. Second, of the rented land in farms, 76 percent was owned by nonfarm operator-landlords. This represented 28 percent of all land in farms. Nonfarm operator-landlords owned and controlled a substantial amount of land not used in farming; we know very little about this land. See U.S. Bureau of the Census, Census of Agriculture, 1969, vol. 5, Special Reports, pt. 2, U.S. Farm Finance (Washington, D.C.: U.S. Government Printing Office, 1974).

11. B. D. Lee Bawden, "The Neglected Human Factor," *American Journal of Agricultural Economics,* vol. 55, December 1973, p. 881.

12. 1974 Catalog of Federal Domestic Assistance, Executive Office of the President and Office of Management and Budget (Washington, D.C.: U.S. Government Printing Office).

13. See, for example: K. C. Schneeberger, J. G. West, D. C. Osborn, and J. Hartman, "Expanding Agricultural Production: The Small Farmer Case," Missouri Agricultural Experiment Station, Journal Series no. 7022; K. C. Schneeberger and J. G. West, "Marginal Farms—A Micro Development Opportunity," *Southern Journal of Agricultural Economics,* vol. 4, no. 1, July 1972, pp. 97–100; Christopher Wardle and Richard N. Boisvert, "Farm and Non-Farm Alternatives for Limited Resource Dairy Farmers in Central New York," A. E. Research 74–6, Cornell University, Ithaca, N.Y., 1974; Howard W. Ladewig and Vance W. Edmondson, "An Interim Evaluation for Low-Income Farmers," Texas A & M University, B-1122 College Station, Tex.; Ronald L. Thompson, "Description and Analysis of Limited Resource Farmers in Michigan," Ph.D. dissertation, Michigan State University, 1975; Robert S. Browne, *Only Six Million Acres: The Decline of Black Owned Land in the Rural South,* Black Economic Research Center, New York, June 1973; and Lester M. Salamon, *Black-Owned Land: Profile of a Disappearing Equity Base,* Report to the Office of Minority Business Enterprises, U.S. Department of Commerce, April 1974. The studies by Browne and Salamon relied on the Census of Agriculture as the primary information base.

14. Calvin L. Beale, *The Revival of Population Growth in Nonmetropolitan America,* U.S. Department of Agriculture, ERS 605, June 1975.

15. Robert S. Browne, *Emergency Land Fund Brochure,* 112 West 20th Street, New York, N.Y. 10027.

chapter 4

A STUDY OF RURAL LANDOWNERSHIP, CONTROL PROBLEMS, AND ATTITUDES OF BLACKS TOWARD RURAL LAND

Leo McGee and Robert Boone

PROBLEM STATEMENT

The decline in black-owned rural land has surfaced as a major issue within the past few years. Developing strategies to arrest this rapid decline in real estate has had high priority on the agenda of concerns in the black community. The land base of all ethnic groups in America is inextricably intertwined with their potential for social, political, and economic progress.

The number of black farmers declined tremendously after World War II. Unlimited job opportunities were available in large urban centers. Farm mechanization forced thousands of tenant farmers out of jobs. In Tennessee alone, black-operated farms dropped from 14,302 in 1959 to 4,930 in 1969.

Some of the reasons cited for the precipitous decline in rural land-ownership include: (1) black migration from the South to northern and western cities, (2) general illiteracy among rural blacks, and (3) chicanery perpetrated under unscrupulous lawyers, land speculators, and county officials.

There was no accurate information available on the actual extent of acreage decline or on the types of title transfer arrangements made by black landowners in Tennessee. Also, no information was available relative to attitudes, opinions, and values held by blacks with respect to rural land. This circumstance was a matter of considerable concern, particularly within the black community, and had generated a number of hypotheses about the causes and remedies. Because of these factors, this study was undertaken to yield factual information on the status and trends of black landownership in Tennessee, to provide information regarding the institutional practices associated with land transfers, and to determine the attitudes held by blacks toward rural land in Tennessee.

QUESTIONS

This study investigates the following specific questions:
1. What is the extent of black-owned rural land in Tennessee?
2. What are the institutional practices associated with rural land transactions?
3. What are the attitudes held by blacks with respect to the ownership of rural land?
4. Have real estate officials been unfair to blacks in land matters, particularly through abusive uses of legal codes?
5. Is there a significant number of blacks who are unaware of real estate legal matters?
6. Are blacks still losing land at an accelerated rate?
7. What are the specific reasons why blacks have lost land?
8. What is the percentage of rural acreage used as a primary and secondary source of family income?
9. Is there a high percentage of black-owned rural land controlled by individuals 55 years of age and older?
10. Are individuals between the ages of 22 and 38 more aggressively seeking ownership of rural acreage?

LIMITATIONS OF THE STUDY

The 1964 Census of Agriculture data revealed that there was a wide variance in the number of black farm operators in the ninety-five counties in the state of Tennessee. This data further indicated that there was a range of zero black farm operators in a number of counties to more than 300 in several others, with the highest number being in the middle and western portions of the state.

To insure participation of an adequate number of black landowners in this study, the research population was geographically limited to three of the counties more densely populated with blacks.

A random sample of 147 landowners was chosen to participate in the study.

DEFINITION OF TERMS

1. *Landowner* refers to a principal owner(s) of a plot of rural land one or more acres in size.
2. *Rural land* refers to acreage located in a community with a population of 2,500 or less.
3. *Farm operator* refers to an individual(s) who utilizes rural acreage as a primary or secondary source of family income. That individual(s) may or may not be the principal owner of the property.
4. *Tenant farmer* refers to an individual(s) who rents rural acreage. The family lives on the property and often pays a portion of or the total amount of the expenses incurred with assets gained from the marketing of produce.
5. *Land transaction* refers to communication between courthouse personnel, land speculators, or real estate officials and the landowner.

METHODOLOGY

RESEARCH SAMPLE

A review of the 1969 Census of Agriculture data revealed that in the ninety-five counties in the state of Tennessee a small percentage did not have black inhabitants who were farm operators, particularly in the eastern portion of the state. The research sample was taken from three of the counties more heavily populated with black farmers, Maury, Fayette, and Haywood.

The researchers were assisted by the Farm Home Administration (FmHA) and Mid Cumberland Region Project in the identification of the 147 black landowners who participated in the study.

INSTRUMENTATION

A thirty-question questionnaire was developed to collect research data. A small section of the instrument was designed to obtain demographic data from subjects. With the exception of the demographic section, the questionnaire was divided into three sections, with ten questions per section.

The questionnaire addressed three areas: "Attitudes of Blacks toward Rural Land," "Perception of Blacks with Respect to Institutional Practices Associated with the Transfer of Rural Land," and "Perception of Blacks with Regard to the Status and Trends of Rural Landownership."

The questionnaire was field-tested in Sumner County, Tennessee. Fifty landowners were administered the questionnaire. The primary purpose of this activity was to improve the readability, understanding, objectivity, and practicality of the instrument.

DATA COLLECTION

A visit was made to the courthouse of each of the target counties to review the record-keeping procedure. This included a visit to the office of the registrar and the county tax assessor. The office of the registrar contained records of property transfers, land acreage, and the amount of money paid for land. The tax assessor's office provided current information on property assessment for tax purposes.

While engaged in the process of field-testing the questionnaire, it became obvious to the researchers that a vast majority of landowners were unable to complete the questionnaire without direct assistance. Consequently, the decision was made to have all questionnaires completed by professionals with training in interviewing. In each county, professionals were employed to administer the questionnaire in an interview-type setting. All were present or former public school teachers. All were given three hours of instruction in interviewing by a psychologist.

The questionnaire was administered on a door-to-door basis to 147 landowners. The first portion of the questionnaire required that subjects provide demographic data which in this case included: sex, age, number of children, value of land, year land was purchased, use of land, marital status, number of acres owned, price paid for land, and employment status. The subjects were instructed to respond to the final thirty questions on a likert-type continuum: strongly agree, agree, strongly disagree, disagree, and no opinion.

ANALYSIS OF DATA

The two primary statistical techniques used to analyze the data in this study were the one-way analysis of variance and percentage.

A total of 147 subjects participated in the study. They were administered a thirty-question questionnaire by trained interviewers. Subjects were also required to provide interviewers with demographic-related information. The questions were divided into three sections, with ten questions to each section that addressed three different topics: Section 1—*Attitudes toward Land;* Section 2—*Perception of Institutional Practices Associated with the Transfer of Rural Land;* Section 3—*Perception of Status and Trends of Rural Landownership.*

The questions in the questionnaire are referred to as "variables" throughout this section. The questionnaire utilized in the study follows:

SECTION 1
ATTITUDES TOWARD LAND

Variables

1. Renting land is as personally self-fulfilling as owning land.
2. Preserving the natural beauty of land is more important than economic benefits.
3. Landownership is not important to my self-image.
4. It is alright to mortgage your land if you pay your bill on time.
5. Ownership of land is becoming more important to individuals in our mobile society.
6. Ownership of land is important to me because it can be passed on to my children.
7. Owning land is important for a personal sense of security.
8. Landownership contributes more to one's feeling of self worth than owning other material goods.
9. One of the best ways of achieving personal status is through landownership.
10. Decisions about who to sell land to should be based upon race.

SECTION 2
PERCEPTION OF INSTITUTIONAL PRACTICE
ASSOCIATED WITH THE TRANSFER OF RURAL LAND
Variables

1. Many blacks have lost their land by illegal means.
2. Most real estate officials make sure that blacks clearly understand legal papers in land transactions prior to signing them.
3. The refusal of mortgage companies to make loans to blacks has contributed significantly to the shortage of black-owned land.
4. Persons in official capacities often work together to gain possession of black-owned rural land.
5. When a landowner dies, real estate officials often make sure that the acreage is evenly divided among relatives.
6. Often individuals mortgage their property to buy food and other necessities, but many eventually lose their property.
7. The present system adequately notifies landowners of the time to pay property taxes.
8. Much land is lost because of the failure of landowners to write wills.
9. Often blacks are forced to sell their land, especially when it is valuable.
10. In order to receive welfare assistance, one has to sell his/her land.

SECTION 3
PERCEPTION OF STATUS AND TRENDS OF RURAL
LANDOWNERSHIP
Variables

1. A sizeable number of individuals lost their property because they failed to meet their mortgage obligations.
2. An increasing number of young people are returning South from northern cities to buy rural land.
3. Most blacks do not have adequate knowledge about the procedures involved in buying and selling land.
4. Due to the changing times, many individuals are holding on to their land.

5. Because of the inability to make land into a profitable investment, many blacks are forced to sell their plots.
6. It is more profitable to own land today than it was ten years ago.
7. Most farmland is not in use; it stands idle.
8. Today, more people are aware of the date their land taxes are
due.
9. Most landowners do not trust real estate officials.
10. Many landowners are unsure of the validness of their deeds.

The acres of rural land owned by the 147 subjects in the target
counties are rather evenly distributed—Fayette, 4,588; Haywood,
3,214; and Maury, 3,555. The total price paid for the 11,327 acres was
$741,185, an average of $65.43 per acre. The subjects estimated that
the acreage is presently worth $1,172,000. The estimated appreciation
price of $430,815 is relatively low since fifty-four subjects purchased
their property before 1966.

It has been reported that blacks often encounter difficulty in purchasing rural land from white owners. The findings in this study may well
corroborate this. Ninety-four, or 64 percent, of the 147 subjects indicated that previous owners of their land were black while only thirty-
seven indicated that the previous owners were white, leaving sixteen
uncertain.

While 90 percent of the subjects believed that there is a trend toward
the purchase of rural land by younger blacks, 93, or 63 percent, of the
147 participants in this study were fifty-five years of age and above.

The table on p. 62 indicates that at the .05 level there was a significant difference in the way different age groups perceived the following
variables: "Most blacks do not have adequate knowledge about the
procedures involved in buying and selling land." The subjects were
divided into four age groups: 0-22, 23-38, 39-54, 55 and above.

Landowners 55 years of age and above indicated more strongly that
owning land was more self-fulfilling than renting. Subjects between the
ages of 23 and 38 were more adamant in their contention that owning
land was important to one's self image. On the other hand, the 55 and
above age group was more confident with regard to their knowledge
about the procedures involved in buying and selling land.

An analysis of variance on variable no. 3:

Most blacks do not have adequate knowledge about the procedures in-
volved in buying and selling land.

Source	D.F.	Sum-of-Squares	Mean Squares	F-Ratio	F-Prob
Between Groups	3	7.578369	2.52612	2.86786	.0388
Within Groups	142	125.0793	.880840		
TOTAL	145	132.6577			

$\overline{X}$ = 2.4 23 – 28
$\overline{X}$ = 2.3 39 – 54
$\overline{X}$ = 1.9 55 & A

In middle-class America the average number of children is approximately two per family. In this study 21 percent, or 32 of the families,
had at least nine children.

Many reasons have been cited for the decline in black landownership.
Ninety-six percent of the subjects felt that land loss was primarily due to
illegal means. Eighty-eight percent attributed black land loss to two
major reasons: the refusal of mortgage companies to make loans to
blacks, and persons in official capacities working together to gain possession of black-owned land.

Widespread illiteracy has historically had an adverse effect on the
quality of life of rural citizens in America. The next three tables may
well lead the reader to infer that illiteracy is prevalent in rural areas.
Ninety percent of the subjects indicated that land loss is due to failure of
blacks to write wills. Ninety-one percent believed blacks were in-
adequately prepared with regard to real estate transactions. Eighty-two
percent felt that uncertainty does exist among black landowners with
respect to the validness of their land deeds.

A large percentage of the subjects reacted favorably to variables that
addressed the tax notification date. Ninety-six percent of the subjects
felt that they were adequately notified of the date to pay property taxes.

While 72 percent of the male subjects agreed that "It is alright to

mortgage your land if you pay your bill on time,'' only 57 percent of the
female subjects agreed to the concept.

It may be safe to conclude that in the families where male figures
have been more dominant and this ''permissive'' attitude more preva
lent, the loss of rural land has been greatest. It is a well-known fact that
those families who mortgage their rural acreage are rarely able to regain
full possession.

Percentages on Variable No. 8:

Much land is lost because of the failure of landowners to write wills.

Category		Number	Percent
Agree		114	90.3
Disagree		11	8.7
	Total	125	100.0

Percentages on Variable No. 3:

*Most blacks do not have adequate knowledge about the procedures
involved in buying and selling land.*

Category		Number	Percent
Agree		126	91.4
Disagree		12	8.6
	Total	138	100.0

Percentages on Variable No. 10:

Many landowners are unsure of the validity of their deeds.

Category		Number	Percent
Agree		105	82.2
Disagree		23	17.8
	Total	128	100.0

FINDINGS AND RECOMMENDATIONS

FINDINGS
1. Blacks generally agree that ownership of rural land is desirable.
2. Black landowners are in dire need of more knowledge regarding real estate legal matters, that is, writing wills, mortgage, foreclosures, heir property, property appraisal, partition sales, tax sales, eminent domain, and so on.
3. A large percentage of black-owned rural land was lost by illegal means, primarily initiated by lawyers, land speculators, and county officials.
4. Females are more likely to show a greater concern for rural land retention than males.
5. A vast majority of black-owned rural land is owned by individuals 55 years of age and above.
6. The failure of mortgage companies to make loans to blacks has contributed significantly to the shortage of black-owned land.
7. Blacks are more likely to purchase rural land from blacks than from whites.
8. Illiteracy among rural blacks has contributed to land loss, primarily because of their inability to effectively negotiate during real estate transactions.
9. Blacks are notified in ample time to pay property taxes.
10. Younger blacks are not aggressively purchasing rural land.
11. "Official" courthouse land records are not always accurate. Discrepancies as to the total acreage owned are common between the offices of the registrar and the county tax assessor. In essence, many blacks do not know how much land they own.
12. Landowners often fail to keep their records current with those kept in the courthouse. As a result, title to land is often found in the name of persons that are deceased.
13. Rural land is still being sold at an alarming rate and often for a very nominal amount. Black rural landowners do not identify with the local "Courthouse Establishment."
14. Blacks often regard persons in official capacities in the courthouse with fear, distrust, and suspicion.
15. Many blacks are unsure of the validity of their deeds.

16. Many blacks lack the financial resources and technical skills needed to transform their land into a profitable investment. Many black landowners are too old and too poor to make their land profitable; therefore, high taxes are causing a constant strain on their income.
17. The millions of blacks who migrated from the South contributed significantly to the decline in black-owned rural land.
18. The Census of Agriculture is an unacceptable research data resource because of the procedure used to record information on black farm-owners and farm operators and because the data are outdated.

RECOMMENDATIONS

As a result of the findings of this study and due to the paucity of research relative to the issue of "Black Rural Land Decline," the following recommendations are made:

1. Extensive research projects should be conducted which cover various aspects of the issue of "Black Rural Land Decline" that are less dependent upon the Census of Agriculture resource data.
2. Institutions of higher education should become more involved in this crucial problem through the initiation of research projects, practica, and seminars that will directly improve the knowledge of black landowners in real estate transactions.
3. Funding agencies should commit more financial resources to support projects dealing with this important issue.
4. A national network should be established to give more attention to the concerns surrounding the issue of "Black Rural Land Decline."
5. The local courthouse staffs should make a greater effort to locate owners of "tax-delinquent property." Advertisements in local as well as major newspapers would allow many heir property owners to rescue tax-delinquent land.

chapter 5

RURAL ACREAGE IN PROMISE LAND, TENNESSEE: A CASE STUDY

Charles Nesbitt

DEMOGRAPHY

The black family's devotion to the development of "community," throughout the more than 110 years of land accumulation and decline in the South following the Civil War, is a very important story. Throughout the history of the black man's existence in America various methods and techniques of self-supporting activity have taken place. However, they very often have gone unrecognized.[1]

The more than one-hundred-year existence of one particular community's fight for life in mid-Tennessee is typical of the countless cases that have taken place. For the most part, historians, geographers, and sociologists have failed to study the tremendously important phenomenon of black existence within self-prescribed community settings. On the other hand, other aspects of their status as landless dependents have been quite prevalent.

Library shelves are filled with studies that extol the very hapless circumstances faced by black people, that stretch across more than four hundred years of life in America.[2] These scholarly works primarily dwell on the negative aspects of black life. While most research in this area gives a good account of ways and means used to control the black man, there is a noticeable void of the blacks' organized reaction.

Particularly omitted are the efforts by blacks to develop their rural neighbors into real communities. Promise Land, Tennessee, depicts the fight for existence by many black rural communities.

Black families have existed on tracts of land in what is called Promise Land since 1870. These four families, consisting of no more than a dozen people who still reside there, have maintained an atmosphere of

2. Due to limited resources, many black farmers are unable to transform their farms into a profitable operation. *Photo by John Cross*

"community" for the more than five hundred individuals who have left. The following gives a demographic perspective of Promise Land, Tennessee:

> *Promise Land, Tennessee, 1881–1979:* Although land in the area was owned by black families prior to 1881 the area was not given its name until that year.

> *Location:* Northern section of Dickson County, mid-Tennessee, Districts 6 and 15: Plots 46, 47, 56, and 57.

> *County seat of government:* Charlotte, located two and one-half miles south. Larger municipality, Dickson, population 21,000, located ten miles to the south.[3]

> *Population:* 500 plus at the height of the community's growth (1900–1935). Presently, only four families consisting of eight adults and a few children/grandchildren live in Promise Land.

> *Land base:* In days past, well over 1,000 acres of farm and timber land, most with natural springs, made up the area. Presently, the four remaining families hold deeds to approximately 50 acres. Some 50 to 60 additional acres are deeded to absentee owners. Most land in the latter category is heir property that is unkept with a good amount in constant jeopardy of public auction due to delinquent taxes.[4]

> *Education:* A public school was operated by the county from 1918 to 1956. A school was organized and staffed by volunteers thirty years prior to the county's financial support. At its peak, the school enrolled over 100 students and employed two teachers for grades one through eight.[5]

EARLY HISTORY, 1870–1930

According to records as kept by the Registrar of Deeds, Dickson County Courthouse, Charlotte, Tennessee, the earliest recorded purchase of land by a black man was consummated January 1, 1870.[6] Thus in a few short years following the Emancipation Proclamation and the Civil War, blacks realized the value of landownership as exemplified in this purchase. Washington Vanleer purchased 14 acres more or less at a cost of $140.[7] This amount, although small by today's standards, represented a substantial commitment. The common rate per acre so set some ten years later "to encourage growth and development," according to editorial accounts, ranged between $1.40 and $3 per acre.[8] Vanleer's rate per acre was a staggering $10, an amount unheard of compared to land deals entered into by white farmers being encouraged to develop the region. It must be assumed that the rights of citizenship that included voting, public education, and, of course, landownership loomed large in the minds of free blacks who insisted that the Freedmen's Bureau come to their aid in 1869–1870.[9]

Although the white political machinery of that time seemingly went to great lengths to prove that recently freed blacks were not interested in the rights of citizenship as provided under the United States and state constitutions, such efforts were proven to be racially motivated or having economic and/or political overtones.[10] A large number of blacks were forced to assume the more docile role of sharecropper through acts of economic and political deceit.[11] When trickery could not be used to keep black farmers dependent, more serious threats and/or actual violence were carried out. The following information as taken from the superintendent of public instruction report for Dickson County in 1870 points up the peril faced by those who dared to instruct blacks in an organized fashion.

> By order of the Grand Cyclops M. M. Hiland, alias Negro Hiland:
> You are hereby notified to disband the school of which you are in
> charge at Jackson Chapel as it is contrary to the wishes of every
> respectable man in the vicinity and an insult to the refinement of
> this community. If this notice fails to effect its purpose, you may
> expect to find yourself suspended by rope with your feet about six
> feet from the terra firma. We hope you will give the same consideration: and in case failure on your part, we intend to carry into
> exercusion [sic] the above plan. Beware! Beware! Beware!!![12]

In spite of the very real attempts to stop transactions that transferred landownership, or activities through which the zeal to acquire property would be developed among blacks in Dickson County, three purchases stand out that proved to be quite important. In addition to the Vanleer tract, Nathan Bowen bought 10 adjoining acres in 1875 for $153.[13] Six years later two tracts somewhat larger than these were sold. Two brothers, John and Arch Nesbitt, made the important purchases of 58 and 25 acres in District 6 outside Charlotte in 1880 and 1881.[14]

A comparison of prices paid by early blacks for land in the area revealed the hard fact that they paid dearly for the property sold to them by whites. Table 5.1 shows that prices paid per acre for land in the area that was to become Promise Land were not significantly different over an eleven-year span of deed dates. The sellers in three of the four cases were different. Neither time nor circumstances over a decade adversely altered the selling prices of land to black people. However, the records show quite a difference in prices paid by white buyers in the same period. Prices paid by whites ranged from government gifts to the ceiling rate of $6 per acre.[15]

All deeds perused were written in longhand and the word "colored" or the abbreviation "col" was inserted in parentheses to differentiate between black and white transactors.

TABLE 5.1   **Black Rural Landownership, 1870–1881 (Dickson County District 6)**

Buyer	No. of Acres	Year Purchased	Purchase Price
Washington Vanleer	14	1870	$140
Nathan Bowen	10	1875	153
Arch Nesbitt	25	1880	153
John Nesbitt	58	1881	400

As evidenced, the zeal to acquire property existed together with other attributes of citizenship, including formal education which was resisted strongly by organized vigilante groups. In *The Negro in Tennessee, 1865–1880,* Alrutheus A. Taylor noted that blacks petitioned the first state convention held after the Civil War in 1865 for an amendment reflecting their citizenship rights. This petitioning process included a great deal of organizational and scholastic work as it contained requests for the franchise, landownership, and educational opportunity as rights befitting the new citizenry.[16]

While no intent is made to suggest that blacks in Dickson County had an easy time in their quest for "full rights" as citizens following the war, some given realities helped in that process. First, moral support resulted from organized efforts in Nashville only fifty miles away which had pressed the issues of freedom in all its forms for former slaves. These bold efforts resulted in several bills being argued in their behalf at the state level of government. Black men in Dickson County gained courage as well as methods and techniques that were used to their advantage. Second, the first governor elected after the war, although a strong believer in slavery, was even more a loyal unionist. William G. Brownlow accepted full emancipation of slaves as a matter of national policy despite his antipathy toward blacks.

The governor's two great aims were to restore the state to the Union under the control of extreme loyalists and to humiliate those whom he considered traitors.[17] To accomplish these purposes, he was fully pre- pared to utilize extreme measures. His first message to the legislature was for the ratification of the proposed Thirteenth Amendment to the federal Constitution. He said in part, "Our state has already shown her hand, and placed herself square upon the record; and I flatter myself that her representatives here assembled are ready for a measure which shall forever exclude slavery from the United States."[18]

The amendment was unanimously ratified by a legislature dominated by Brownlow's hand-picked lawmakers. This act paved the way for more favorable legislation regarding citizenship rights of blacks in Ten- nessee much sooner than could have otherwise been expected. Black groups both in and out of the capital, following the lead given to them by their chief executive, continued an organized effort aimed at rights of citizenship not uncommon throughout the South immediately following the Civil War. The results of legislation and the executive loyalist in government, as well as the Freedmen's Bureau, the Anti-Slavery Soci- ety, and religious groups, were a very encouraging push for freedom's rewards by black citizens in mid-Tennessee. Altercations between blacks and whites were common during the period immediately follow- ing the war.

The native whites resented the efforts of those who tried to give the black man political and civic responsibility. Throughout the state vio- lence erupted on numerous occasions in which both blacks and whites were slaughtered.[19] A number of fierce battles occurred between blacks and whites in connection with the elections from 1868 throughout the 1870s. The counties of Pulaski, Marshall, Williamson, and Maury, in addition to Dickson County, witnessed violence between the races especially during the months leading up to elections. Blacks were in fact so demanding in the area that became Promise Land that front-page newspaper space was given their stand in 1868.[20]

The articles ran for a week with the same lead: "There are in Dickson County a class of colored men who stand up for their rights. . . ." They referred to an altercation at the Cumberland Furnace precinct (seven miles from Promise Land) where a group of whites had tried to compel several scores of blacks to vote against Governor Brownlow's regime. The blacks refused to vote at all until they had gone home and returned with loaded muskets. A fight ensued and after men on both sides were wounded the whites, who were outnumbered, fled, whereupon the blacks voted as they pleased.[21]

Another cause of violence and strained race relations was the educational system. Much emphasis was placed on education for the black man by the Freedmen's Bureau Educational Division operating throughout the South following the war.[22] The most objectionable portion of the bureau's program was its aim to educate blacks and whites in the same schools. Equally objectionable was the subject matter taught to blacks, which many white groups reasoned would foment discontent and dissatisfaction among blacks. Schools were established for blacks with funds supplied by the Freedmen's Bureau at Charlotte while a minister conducted classes at Cumberland Furnace. According to the bureau not enough black children were living in the area between these sites to warrant a school.

The relentless and brave efforts of blacks in Dickson County and indeed in all of mid-Tennessee eased the burdens of living in rural areas. Influential whites had to change from the aristocratic methods of antebellum politics to unionization. Poor whites were, for a time, forced into a new role of recognition of the black man. The long-range counter-result, of course, were Jim Crow laws enacted in the legislature, and fiendish Ku Klux Klan activity in the countryside. Previous to such organized white reaction to Reconstruction, however, blacks in Dickson County had received some of the attributes of citizenship that included land and a will to stand up for their rights. Although the sustaining right to the franchise and black testimony used in courts of law against whites were quickly abolished with the dreaded Black Laws, and while their purchases were valid only when witnessed by whites, mid-Tennessee blacks bought land as a first priority of citizenship whenever possible. In Dickson County in general and Districts 6 and 16 in particular the few black people discussed earlier had settled via land purchases in the area soon to be named Promise Land.

According to black verbal histories, the name Promise Land was given to the area in 1881 by a black man, John Nesbitt. The story goes that two brothers, John and Arch Nesbitt, were allowed to purchase land due to their service in the Union army. They were so elated that on a survey of their property they called it "The Promised Land from the Federal Government." The name stuck and was proudly acclaimed as the fulfilled promise of the Union by admirers in Dickson, Charlotte, and Cumberland Furnace.[23] At this point in time, although numerous blacks lived in communities only two and seven miles away, very few blacks ventured to Promise Land. Population figures taken from the Dickson County Census placed the Negro population at 1,677 in 1870, 2,003 in 1880, and 2,919 in 1900.[24] With only 2,003 blacks living in all of the county, a span of 486 square miles, and given the fact that iron furnaces were operated at Cumberland Furnace and Dickson, the tendency not to settle in Promise Land immediately is understandable. The Cumberland Furnace iron works situated seven miles north employed more than one hundred black men who together with wives and children made up a population of over 350 people. In Dickson the furnaces were not so large but other opportunities for work caused blacks to swell that town's population as well.[25]

The coming spurt of black settlement in Promise Land (1880–1920) was primarily due to several reasons. The area had established residents among its proud property owners: (1) Vanleer, 14 acres since 1870; (2) Bowen, 10 acres since 1875; and (3) the Nesbitt brothers, 25 and 58 acres in 1880 and 1881. The Nesbitts gave legitimacy to the area because, in addition to naming it, they donated land on which a school and church were later built. Perhaps the most important reason for black movement into the area was the news of the state's plans to build a major road to connect Nashville and Clarksville that would cut right through Promise Land.[26] Concomitantly, the railroad had laid plans to build a rail-line spur from Vanleer to Cumberland Furnace and Dickson. All of this activity, coupled with the long twelve- and fifteen-hour days men worked within the hot dirty iron works, roused the wonderings of blacks who were living in company-owned shacks around Dickson and

Cumberland Furnace. According to verbal stories handed down by black forefathers, people became very discouraged by the treatment suffered under hard-driving white iron foremen and managers. Very little time for social, religious, or educational activities could be had among the "slave-like conditions around those furnace towns," according to one interviewee.[27] However, work was steady and the pay the best in the area, so the furnace towns never suffered a shortage of able-bodied men. The work force was cut considerably following World War I and the families out of work began to sharecrop with whites and at least one black man in the Promise Land vicinity. Some black men traveled the fourteen-mile round trip to Cumberland Furnace on horseback or in wagons. The end result of all this activity was a buildup of Promise Land inhabitants that saw more land purchases, a school, and church services of three Christian denominations: Methodist Episcopal (on land donated by the Nesbitts), African Methodist Episcopal, and Baptist (who used the same building).

Because Promise Land was never incorporated and there was no town post office or elected officials, exact population data were not kept and recorded separately. However, the community's growth can be seen in deed books kept by the Recorder of Deeds and Tax Assessor in the county seat of Charlotte. From 1881 to 1930 black landownership rose from three families owning some 100 acres to more than twenty-five different family names that either owned land or lived on heir property tracts that totaled over 1,000 acres. Deeds to these plots are recorded in the Dickson County Courthouse in Charlotte. The different family names are authentic as per verbal testimonies given by residents and former residents of the area who range in age from thirty-seven to ninety-one years.[28]

LAND DECLINE, 1930–1978

Perhaps the most significant set of factors that contributed directly to the sharp decline in black landownership in the Promise Land area centers around economics. Without a doubt, a vast majority of blacks left that section of Dickson County seeking employment. Several differently worded reasons were given; however, when analyzed, they all reflect a strong economic basis. The following answers have been recorded from the verbal testimonies of former property owners or their

heirs when questioned as to why they or their relatives left Promise
Land:

> To find work and make some money.
> To get away from my debts.
> To support my family.
> Because my (uncle, aunt, sister, brother, or a friend) had left
> and asked me to follow.
> I couldn't farm the land without money for tools and seed.[29]

Every answer reflects directly on the need for finances in an amount
to sustain a family or an individual. The reasons given for every instance of movement from the area were precipitated by a felt need to
earn a better living. The overwhelming majority of those who joined the
migration paths north obtained jobs mostly in the auto and steel industries of Ohio, Michigan, and Indiana. Their patterns of movement followed these three general routes primarily because another close relative
or friend had paved the way.

Black farmers who owned land could not make it productive without
the kinds of help being received by their white counterparts. Although
Cooperative Extension has provided a valuable service to white farmers
since the passage of the Smith-Lever Act in 1914, blacks did not even
know of, much less receive help from, a "County Agent." The various
resources that were supposed to be available to all farmers via federal,
state, and county cooperatives never became a reality for the black
farmers and homeowners of Promise Land. The government through
exclusion and discrimination practices of the state-based Cooperative
Extension Service, at both the agency and employee levels, forced
blacks to abandon their lands.

The various practices of Jim Crow that advanced poor whites and
penalized blacks were common among the governmental servants of the
public trust. The many instances of undesirable land sales resulted in a
great many lost acres of black property. All sales that were made due to
tax difficulties, cases where one family member imposed his/her will
upon others to sell, or where land was sold at prices below the market
value were termed undesirable.

Dickson County Register of Deeds records show instance after instance a recognizable factor in black land sales—the large white landowner whose property was adjacent to that being sold. Such purchases were further made at public auction prices or settled with the

owners prior to the actual county sale.[30]

These unwritten histories that are not a part of the actual deed transactions of land purchased by whites from blacks in Promise Land are representative of the kind of undesirable sales that transpired: (1) A white buyer bought out one of several relatives who in turn persuaded others to sell shares until controlling interest was outside the family. With family members living elsewhere it became fairly easy to purchase the total tract; (2) To stay out of jail on trumped-up charges or exaggeration of the penalty for minor ones, black landowners mortgaged large acres of land to white businessmen and farmers. The total or parcels of tracts were lost when the note came due and could not be paid; (3) In one case an elderly woman mortgaged several prime acres to her former white employer. The black landowner in this case had worked as a live-in maid for the family for years. After becoming terminally ill she willed the property to her white employer for taking care of her until death.[31] These stories can be multiplied many times over. The end result of all the land dealings, when coupled with some very major national events over a period of time, amounted to major declines in black holdings.

The population of Promise Land decreased considerably following two major events that affected the total country and a third factor which was a more natural occurrence. The stock market crash in 1929 and the resulting Depression forced many people to leave between 1929 and 1934. Some who left during this time returned with the more prosperous economic programs under President Roosevelt's New Deal. Outmigration slowed considerably until World War II temporarily took large numbers of black males from the farms between 1940 and 1945. Even though some young men moved back with their families or even made separate efforts toward productive farming after the Great Depression and World War II, a third factor had begun to erode Promise Land's population.

The second and third generations of Promise Land citizens did not harbor the same feelings that kept their parents and grandparents wed to the land. As the older first-time deed holders died leaving their respective property to family members who had become quite scattered both physically and emotionally the following resulted: an inability to reach agreement to keep the property intact, delinquent taxes, court-appointed sales, vulnerability to larger white farmers and land developers, and mortgage foreclosures.

By the mid-1950s abandoned houses dotted the vast geographic land-scape of Promise Land. Family heads of households were commuting from Dickson, Clarksville, and Nashville by day and weekends to fac-tory jobs. At least two husbands actually worked in Ohio coming home twice yearly, at Christmas and during summer vacation, to be with their families.[32] The end result of all this commuting was that most families reached the decision to leave Promise Land to be near their relatives and make a living at the same time. As indicated earlier whites continued to buy up black land in opportunistic fashion to the total disadvantage of the community.

The population continued to dwindle and dropped to such a low point that church services that had been held each week in two different buildings were held only monthly in one. The county school which had operated in the community on property deeded by a black landowner closed in 1956.[33] Families remaining in the area were now forced to allow their children to be bused to Charlotte and Dickson for classes. The useless building, which at the height of its service accommodated two teachers and over sixty students in addition to all social events, is analogous to conditions that have beset black people wherever they have lived in this country. Although the strategies used to deny black inde-pendence may have been different in Dickson County than in other places, the end result proved to be the same. Blacks were not made to enter into sharecropping agreements at gunpoint in Charlotte and Prom-ise Land, but they did indeed sharecrop. Black landowners generally were not forced off their land by night riders under the cover of sheets in darkness, but were forced off through a coercive system of legal and illegal manipulations.[34] Without a doubt the government at all levels participated in these negative undertakings at the expense of black land-owners.

What happened to black people of Promise Land was not an isolated incident; it has been repeated in hundreds of locations throughout the South. History is full of evidence that shows how the land lost by blacks in small and large amounts has reached over 9,000,000 rural acres.[35] The story of the more than 1,000 acres lost by Promise Land citizens is very representative of the numerous cases that when totaled make up the vast losses on a national scale. What will happen as a result of this information being assembled in print remains to be seen. One can only hope that giant humanistic strides have been taken to halt the practice today. The many blacks elsewhere who have suffered together with those of Promise Land deserve nothing less as a conciliatory gesture from the interpreters and enforcers of the laws that govern all citizens.

NOTES

1. The most fully developed studies of the black community and white responses to it can be found in George Davis and Fred Donaldson, *Blacks in the United States* (Boston: Houghton Mifflin, 1975); Leonard Freed, *Black on White America* (New York: Grossman Publishers, 1967); and August Meier and Elliott Rudwick, *The Making of Black America* (New York: Atheneum, 1969).

2. The following references represent major works that describe the perils of being black in America. Peter I. Rose, *Slavery and its Aftermath* (Chicago: Atherton Press, 1972); Donald I. Warren, *Black Neighborhoods* (Ann Arbor: University of Michigan Press, 1975).

3. General Highway Map of Dickson County, Tennessee, Department of Transportation, Bureau of Planning, Office of Research and Planning, Transportation Building, Nashville, Tenn., 1973.

4. Recorded interviews with present Register of Deeds, Dickson County; former and present residents of Promise Land, May 1976.

5. Minutes of the Dickson County Board of Education meetings, July 29, 1918, June 18, 1928, and May 5 and 6, 1956; Office of Superintendent, Charlotte, Tenn., May 1976.

6. Deed Book N, Register of Deeds, Courthouse, Charlotte, Tenn., 1870, p. 603.

7. Ibid.

8. *Nashville Banner*, May 1880; T. C. Morris in *Dickson County Press*, August 2, 1886; Clarksville semi-weekly *Tobacco Leaf Chronicle*, April 22, 1881.

9. Barnum to Lt. Col. James Thompson, Asst. Comm. of Bureau of Refugees, Freedmen, and Abandoned Lands, in Henry L. Swint, ed., "Reports from Educational Agents of the Freedman's Bureau in Tennessee, 1865-1870," *Tennessee Historical Quarterly* 1, 1942, p. 63.

10. Thomas B. Alexander, *Political Reconstruction in Tennessee* (Nashville: Vanderbilt Press, 1950), p. 249.

11. Ibid., pp. 249-50.

12. Robert E. Carlew, *A History of Dickson County* (Dickson, Tenn.: Tennessee Historical Commission and Dickson County Historical Society, 1956), p. 110.

13. Deed Book Q, Register of Deeds, Courthouse, Charlotte, Tenn., 1875, p. 605.

14. Ibid.; Book R, 1880, pp. 7–8; Book S, 1881, pp. 180–81.

15. Review of various deed books kept by Register of Deeds, Dickson County Courthouse, Charlotte, Tenn., 1870 to 1885.

16. Alrutheus A. Taylor, *The Negro in Tennessee, 1865–1880* (Spartanburg, S.C.: Reprint Co., 1974), p. 2.

17. Ibid., p. 6.

18. Ibid., p. 7.

19. For one of the most complete accounts see testimony taken by the Joint Select Committee to inquire into the condition of affairs in the Late Insurrectionary States, 13 vols. (Washington, D.C., 1872). Volume 13 includes testimony taken in Tennessee. This report is commonly known as the Ku Klux Conspiracy.

20. *Nashville Daily Press and Times*, March 13, 16, 25, 26, and 31, 1868.

21. Ibid., March 31, 1868.

22. For a detailed discussion of the work of northern teachers in the entire South, see Henry L. Swint, *The Northern Teacher in the South, 1862–1870* (Nashville: Vanderbilt University Press, 1941).

23. Interview with Charlie Nesbitt, age 85, former Promise Land resident, June 1976; his father and uncle were major landowners in the community that gave land for a school and the first church in 1901.

24. Census data, Dickson Chamber of Commerce, reports for 1870, 1880 and 1900, Public Library, Dickson, Tenn.

25. Robert E. Carlew, *A History of Dickson County* (Dickson, Tenn.: Tennessee Historical Commission and Dickson County Historical Society, 1956), p. 35.

26. Ibid., p. 38.

27. Interview with Josie Garrett, age 91, former Cumberland Furnace and Promise Land resident, June 1976.

28. Various interviews with residents and former residents of Promise Land (see notes 23 and 27); additional interviews with Ernest Nesbitt, age 63; Dee Langford, age 85; Robert Gilbert, age 71; Hubert Thompson, age 58. Interviewed as empirical data-gathering technique for this book in May and June 1976.

29. Ibid.

30. Perusal of deed books showing land purchases where blacks sold to whites, 1929–1950, Courthouse, Charlotte, Tenn., 1976.

31. Information supplied by Ernest Nesbitt and supported by Dee Langford in interviews at different times at Columbus, Ohio, and Detroit, Mich., 1976.

32. Information supplied by Lizzie Edmondson and Essie Gilbert, current Promise Land residents, May 1976.

33. Tom T. Sugg, report of the Superintendent of Schools, Dickson County Public School System, June 1956, p. 11.

34. See note 30.

35. Anthony Griggs, "How Blacks Lost 9,000,000 Acres of Land," *Ebony,* October 1974, p. 97.

chapter 6

BLACK RURAL LAND DECLINE AND POLITICAL POWER

William E. Nelson, Jr.

BLACK LAND AS A POLITICAL RESOURCE

The relationship between black landownership and political power is one that has received far too little attention in the analysis of the social, economic, and political position of blacks in American society. A number of studies have pointed out the unique status of blacks as victims of racial and class exploitation in America.[1] These studies, however, have generally failed to emphasize the critical importance of the landless status of black people as a pivotal aspect of white domination and control. The denial of an equity base in landownership has consistently been at the heart of black economic impoverishment and political powerlessness in America. In a society based on capitalism, landownership becomes an essential and unalterable prerequisite for economic development and the exercise of substantial political influence. The continuous insulation of blacks from those aspects of the marketplace wherein land can be obtained and translated into significant capital has been the sine qua non of American domestic colonialism. As James Turner has pointed out, "Without control over any significant portion of the area they occupy, not having ownership of any capital instruments or means of production, black people are not simply oppressed but are the victims of super exploitation."[2]

The exercise of substantial influence by any group in the American political process requires control over, and effective utilization of, a number of important resources; one of the most important is economic wealth.[3] Limited black control over land has deprived the black community of a major source of wealth in this country. This fact has, in turn, had a host of serious consequences for the effective mobilization of black strength in the political process. Economic dependence induced by the absence of capital-producing institutions has robbed the black community of the ability to make independent political decisions. Black leaders have frequently been so reliant on outside white support they have become virtual political hostages. Similarly, black organizational efforts have been constrained by clientage relations that require white involvement and control.[4] Under such circumstances, policymaking in the black community fundamentally reflects preferences imposed by whites on blacks by virtue of their control of the means of economic survival.

Economic dependence has also had a dampening effect on black political activism. In this respect, the issue of black landownership looms especially large. Land-owning blacks who possess a certain measure of independence tend to be far more inclined toward involvement in political activities (such as voting and civil rights protests) than blacks who are landless and economically insecure.[5] Thus blacks in Holmes County, Mississippi, where more than one hundred independent black farm families reside, have been more deeply involved in the struggle for civil rights than any other identifiable group of black citizens in the state. Their ownership of land has conveyed to them a sense of power and personal security. Landless blacks in Mississippi lack the sense of confidence and personal stake which flows from property ownership. Consequently, they have been far less responsive to formal and informal attempts to stimulate their active involvement in the political process.

Finally, because of its dependent economic status, the black community's impact as a bargaining force in the political process has been substantially diluted. Operating in the political system from a low resource base, the black community is in a poor position to achieve a positive response to its claims from elected officials and public bureaucracies in the face of counterclaims from groups possessing an abundance of economic resources. Politicians typically strive to satisfy the desires of those groups most critical to their survival in office. Without independent economic resources, the black community cannot deliver the money, the technical expertise, and the command over the electoral process that politicians demand as quid pro quo for their administrative intervention. Bureaucrats are equally sensitive to the delivery and resource capacity of their potential clients.[6] Blacks, being heavily dependent on public benefits, are more likely to be the objects of bureaucratic control than the chief manipulators of bureaucratic decision-making.

In sum, black-owned land capable of being usefully developed or converted into capital constitutes an immensely valuable political resource. If used correctly, a black land base could be critical to the political empowerment of the black community. The absence of such a base, on the other hand, can have a crippling effect on the mobilization potential of the black community in the political process.

THE FAILURE OF BLACK LAND REFORM

The organic connection between black landownership and political power finds its clearest expression in the experience of blacks in the South. Ever since their arrival in America as slaves, southern blacks have been tied to the soil. In the main, they have worked in agriculture as the servants of white landowners, rather than as private farmers with substantial personal investments in rural land. The landless status of southern blacks can be traced directly to the failure of the land-reform movement during Reconstruction. Under legislation drafted in 1864, by Congressman George Washington Julian of Indiana and Congressman Thaddeus Stevens of Pennsylvania, land confiscated or forfeited in the South was to be given to men who served in the Union army, including blacks. Applying the provisions of this act specifically to the condition of black laborers, Stevens proposed that each adult male freedman be given 40 acres so that he could establish for himself a family farm and gain a foothold in the American economy.[7] Unfortunately, these plans for the redistribution of southern lands were never carried out. Although the proposed federal legislation passed in the House of Representatives, it failed in the Senate. In the absence of federal policy undergirded by federal pressure, only limited amounts of confiscated federal property passed into black hands. One notable example of such land granted to blacks was the experiment in which land owned by Confederate planters in the Sea Islands—located between Savannah, Georgia, and Charleston, South Carolina—was turned over to blacks in individual small plots. The only other significant experiment of this sort was one in which several plantations formerly owned by Confederate army officers were turned over to blacks in Davis-Bend, Mississippi, near Vicksburg.[8]

The failure of the land-reform movement during Reconstruction left the black population largely without a land base. In some states outside the deep South, blacks did enjoy some notable success in purchasing small parcels of farmland. For example, in Norfolk and Princess Ann, Virginia, white planters sold land to freedmen "who rapidly became a respectable solid tax-paying class."[9] Blacks in Gloucester County, Virginia, owned more than 500 acres of land in 1865. In 1880, 195 blacks in this county owned approximately 2,300 acres.[10] These examples do not represent the typical experience of blacks seeking to realize their ambitions of becoming individual farmers. Racial prejudice and the lack of money constituted insuperable obstacles to landownership for the bulk of the black population. As a substitute for landownership, most blacks became tenants or sharecroppers on plantations owned by whites. In many instances they were reduced to peonage, a condition that did not markedly differ from their former status under slavery.

Although data on black landownership are sketchy and incomplete, the information available strongly supports the proposition that blacks have never controlled more than a small percentage of the total land acreage in the South. W.E.B. Du Bois estimates that blacks held 3 million acres in 1875, 8 million in 1890, and 12 million in 1900.[11] The peak year of black landownership was 1910; in this year blacks owned an estimated 15 million acres. Since that time, black landownership has steadily declined. It is estimated that in 1969 blacks owned less than 6 million acres, representing 79,000 owner-operated farms and about 17,000 tenant-operated farms.[12]

DEMISE OF BLACK POLITICAL POWER

The underrepresentation of blacks in southern landownership is, in large measure, a reflection of the powerlessness of blacks in southern politics. The political power of southern blacks has been in a shattered and diluted state since the 1890s and the onset of the era of disfranchisement. Through the use of a number of devices including constitutional reform, the poll tax, the literacy test, the grandfather clause, and the white primary, southern state governments were extraordinarily successful in stripping the black population of its voting rights. During the era of Reconstruction blacks had voted in strong numbers; through the method of bloc voting, blacks had in fact succeeded in electing black politicians to a variety of local, state, and national offices. Upon their ascension to power and dominance in the wake of the removal of federal troops from the South after 1876, white officials turned against the black community with a vengeance, nullifying black voting rights through every means at their disposal.[13] The success of the disfranchisement campaign can be readily seen in statistics which show that, for example, in New Orleans between 1896 and 1908, the black electorate was reduced from 14,000 to 408. Across the state of Louisiana, black registration dropped by 96 percent within two years after the adoption of the New Louisiana Constitution, including its disfranchisement provisions, in 1898. During this same period, black registration in Alabama had dropped to less than 3,000 (or 2 percent) of a black male voting-age population of 181,471.[14] The most important consequence of this emasculation of black voting strength was the subordination of the black community to the white community, and the forging of patterns of economic and political dependency.

> With the full application of doctrines of white supremacy in the 1890s in the creation of the traditional system, the Negro community became the truncated off-shoot of the white community and was heavily dependent on it. Most of the business, professional, political and social activities common to organized social life took place in the white community and little or none among Negroes. Negro political life was almost nonexistent; what little did exist was controlled by whites. Negro business never developed and prospered as once hoped; it remained confined largely to small business such as grocery stores and funeral parlors; in large centers other businesses such as insurance companies developed.[15]

The greatest potential for black economic development lay in the Blackbelt where blacks were concentrated in significant numbers and had a long history of agricultural productivity. However, it was in these Blackbelt counties where blacks often constituted numerical majorities that efforts to deny them voting rights were most intense. Pressure for disfranchisement surfaced first and most vigorously in Blackbelt counties in Mississippi and Alabama where blacks outnumbered whites. In the middle of the 1950s blacks continued to face an intractable white power structure intent on using every available means to keep them from rising to power through the electoral process. Blacks and whites in Fayette County, Tennessee, had lived a fairly peaceful existence until 1959 when the black majority began to demand voting rights. Seizing

on their primary instrument of power—control over the economy including a near monopoly of landownership—whites launched a vicious
campaign of retaliation and harassment. Black field hands who sought
to register to vote were discharged from their jobs and kicked out of
their homes on white-owned land. Local merchants refused to trade with
potential black voters. Insurance policies held by blacks seeking to
register were either canceled or not renewed. Eventually, the economic
plight of blacks became so severe that a "tent city" was erected to
house those who had been evicted, and a nationwide campaign for relief
was launched.[16]

In Alabama, a bold attempt by the Alabama legislature was made in
1957 to block the emergence of majority rule in Macon County by
redrawing the boundaries of the city of Tuskegee in such a way that 420
black voters were placed outside the city limits, leaving only 10 black
voters inside the city limits. No white voters were affected by the
gerrymander. Consequently, through legislative fiat, whites in Tuskegee were transformed from an electoral minority to an overwhelming
electoral majority, and black political influence in the county was dealt
a fatal blow.[17] In 1961 this blatant act of political manipulation was
nullified by a federal court decision declaring the 1957 gerrymander
illegal.

At the same time the Tuskegee gerrymander issue was being hotly
contested, blacks in Macon County were engaged in a protracted struggle to get Governor John Patterson to appoint members to the Macon
County Board of Registrars so that blacks could register to vote. Fearing
a total takeover of county government by the black majority, Governor
Patterson resisted all attempts by blacks to get a board appointed for
more than a year and a half.[18] In the final analysis, Patterson consented
to reactivate the board only when it became clear that if he did not, the
federal government would step in to register blacks under the 1960
voting rights act.

There is good reason to believe that white antipathy to black political
participation in the South is based, in part, on the fear that a powerful
black electorate will use its political influence to deprive the white
population of its near-monopoly of landownership. In Greene County,
Alabama, efforts by the Nation of Islam to purchase 3,600 acres of
farmland stirred an extraordinary emotional reaction by the indigenous
white population. The clear impression left by this event is that local
whites were less concerned about the religious affiliations of the group's

members than that they were black people seeking to purchase extensive valuable real estate. More revealing, however, is the case of the quest for land in Mississippi by the Republic of New Africa (RNA).

The RNA is a black nationalist organization founded in Detroit in 1968. It has as its primary objective the building of an independent black state in a 20,000-square-mile area along the Mississippi River from Memphis to New Orleans.[19] The bulk of this territory lies in the state of Mississippi. Informally, the area is known in black nationalist circles as the Kush District. In 1970 the headquarters of the RNA moved from Detroit to the Kush area (first to New Orleans, then to Jackson) to begin the process of purchasing land upon which the new black state would be built. When local whites heard of the active efforts by the RNA to establish an independent land base in Mississippi they were horrified. Yielding to local pressure the black Hinds County farmer who originally sold the land to the RNA abrogated the contract. The state then filed an injunction against the RNA prohibiting the organization from reoccupying the land site.[20]

Throughout the RNA's presence in Mississippi, the organization had encountered harassment and intimidation by the local police and the FBI. Harassment of the RNA reached a climax on August 18, 1971, when local police and FBI officers raided the RNA headquarters at 6:30 A.M. on the pretext of looking for a black fugitive. When RNA members did not respond to orders to come out of the headquarters in sixty seconds, tear gas was fired and shots rang out. When the smoke had cleared, one police officer was dead and another policeman and an FBI agent were wounded. Eleven members of the RNA were tried and convicted on charges ranging from murder to assault. Four RNA members remain incarcerated; the others are free pending appeal of their convictions. What the experience of the RNA in Mississippi clearly demonstrates is that whites are highly intolerant of black nationalist efforts (or those of any other blacks) to peacefully establish a land base for the black community. Unquestionably, southern whites possess keen insight into the importance of land as a resource for a people struggling for economic survival and advancement.

BLACK POWERLESSNESS AND BLACK LAND DECLINE

The absence of effective black political power in the South has a number of important implications for the problem of black land decline.

First, the inability of blacks to compete in the southern political process has meant that they have had no influence on federal and local land policies. Federal land programs have been primarily oriented to help large farmers, not small. As a consequence of this one-sided emphasis, blacks, whose land is concentrated in small farms, have found it difficult to maintain viable farm operations and have been forced to sell out to white land developers. Federal programs obstensibly designed to help small, poor farmers have been woefully inadequate. Thus provisions in the 1964 Economic Opportunity Act providing financial assistance to poor farmers which call for loans rather than grants have had little effect in helping poor farmers improve their farms or stave off the omnipresent menace of bankruptcy. As Robert Browne has observed, without the grant assistance, poor farmers have not been able to satisfy legislative requirements that there be reasonable assurance of repayment.[21] The result has been that the bulk of government loans has gone to white farmers with incomes well above the poverty level.

Second, the underrepresentation of blacks in key administrative positions has encouraged collusion between public officials and private investors to swindle black people out of their land. A sizable proportion of the land lost by blacks to whites has been taken through tax sales conducted by city and county governments. These governmental bodies gain possession of the land after black tax accounts become delinquent. In many instances tax sales amount to no more than grand theft of black land. Taking advantage of the lack of knowledge and sophistication of black landowners, white officials have often manufactured tax delinquency circumstances through unethical and illegal means. Black property owners have complained, for example, that their land has been taken despite the fact they never received a tax bill or were never given a full understanding of the status of their accounts.[22] Similar acts of official misconduct have frequently resulted in the loss of land through partition sales and foreclosures. Almost without exception, behind the initiation of official action against black landowners designed to take away their property stands a white private investor or firm eagerly waiting to buy the disputed property as soon as its title is transferred back into the public domain. If blacks were represented in significant numbers in such positions as sheriff, county assessor, and other key offices, much of the agony attendant to the problem of black land decline could probably have been avoided. However, because they have lacked a foothold in the electoral process, blacks have exercised little influence over the private negotiations resulting in the public confiscation of black land for private purposes.

Finally, the continuing poverty of black rural communities accruing from white political domination and control has been a major factor underlying black outmigration to the urban North, and the concomitant dislocation of blacks from important land in the South. Black control over city and county government would have the effect of shifting governmental priorities toward the satisfaction of critical black needs. If such a shift were to be realized, the urban North would be far less attractive to the millions of blacks who have abandoned their southern mooring since World War II in search of economic advantages and a more conducive political climate. Support for this assertion can be found in the pattern of reverse black migration to Atlanta in the wake of the spectacular growth of black political control in recent years. Black-controlled governments committed to protecting and advancing the rights of black people could go a long way toward stemming the trend of black outmigration and land decline.

BLACK ELECTORAL GAINS AND BLACK LANDOWNERSHIP

The passage of the Voting Rights Act in 1965 is the pivotal factor underlying the expectation that southern blacks will be able to expand their equity base through increased influence in the political process. As a consequence of the passage of this act, the greatest gains by blacks in terms of electoral success have been made in the South. In 1974 there were 1,609 elected black officials in the South; this figure represented 54 percent of all elected black officials in the country. Thus, in a few short years black governmental representation has been brought into greater harmony with the black population.

What impact have these developments had on black landownership? There is no evidence that gains made by blacks in the South have resulted in dramatic breakthroughs in the expansion and protection of the black equity base. The reasons for this are several. First, despite the gains that have been made, blacks are still seriously underrepresented in public offices in the South. One study conducted in 1973 suggested that blacks had political control in few of the twenty-six counties of which they comprised a majority of the electorate.[23] Further, this study showed that in only five of fifty counties in which blacks were a majority of the voting population did they have majority control over county commissions.[24] There were, in addition, 160 southern cities with black majorities that had white mayors; in 111 of these cities no blacks held public offices.[25]

Second, elected black officials tend to be concentrated at the town, village, and city levels. Of the positions held at the municipal level, 93 percent are seats on city councils.[26] Most of the councilmen come from small towns; only 10 percent are elected from cities with 100,000 or more residents.[27] In local politics many of the most powerful positions are located at the county level. Blacks have not made significant headway in breaking the white monopoly on county positions. The more powerful and important the position, the more likely the occupant of the office will be white. In 1973, there were only three black county sheriffs, four black tax collectors or assessors, one black treasurer, and one black school superintendent.[28] All nine of these officials won their offices in counties where voters are predominantly black. As has been discussed, black control over positions such as county sheriff, tax collector, and tax assessor is an essential prerequisite for the eradication of the kind of chicanery by whites underlying the steady decline of black landownership.

Third, black officials in black majority counties lack the fiscal resources to launch an aggressive attack against many of the problems affecting black land possessions. The resource base of these counties is so devastatingly low that elected black officials encounter great difficulty in simply attempting to provide basic services; they have no resources to fight legal battles in the court to save their constituents from rapacious whites intent on stealing their land.[29]

Fourth, whites have shown great skill in diluting the power of elected black officials and circumventing their offices in their efforts to continue to exercise inordinate influence. Among the tactics most frequently used are gerrymandering and the consolidation of election districts to prevent more than a few token blacks from gaining access to public office, fear and recrimination as a weapon to frighten blacks from the polls, and the holding of private caucuses by white officials to which their black colleagues are not invited.[30]

Fifth, gains at the local level have not been translated into expanded black influence at the state and national levels. Black influence over state and federal policies is practically nonexistent. What the black community faces is a system of white power permeating the entire federal system. At the present time, blacks do not possess sufficient strength to neutralize the deleterious effects of this national system of white power.

Sixth, black electoral gains have not resulted in a significant generation of legal and technical expertise of the kind required to assist black landowners in protecting their investments and making them profitable. Some studies show, in fact, that the black community may be losing ground in this respect. The dramatic decline in the black rural population has, for example, had an enormously corrosive impact on agricultural training programs in black colleges. Severe financial shortages, coupled with declining enrollments, have greatly undermined the capacity of these programs to offer technical assistance to small black farmers.[31]

One shining star in the area of technical assistance is the Emergency Land Fund sponsored by the Black Economic Research Center. This agency is involved not only in providing technical assistance, but in financially underwriting the cost of keeping troubled black land holdings viable and in black hands. However, much more needs to be done in this area to keep the 6 million acres now owned by blacks from dwindling to 600 in the next six years.

CONCLUSION

The absence of a viable equity base has been costly to the black community both economically and politically. Black dependency on white economic support has served to rob the black community of its autonomous decision-making potential. Further, without the advantage of a steady income and personal property in which they can take pride, many poverty-stricken blacks have been unable to develop a serious interest in political activity. At the same time, black organizational efforts—both political and economic—have been crippled by the lack of a sufficient equity base to keep them independently viable.

Economically, the black community has lost billions of dollars in wages and profits that would go to black workers and owners if blacks owned land in proportion to their numbers. Underrepresentation of blacks in landownership can, without question, be translated into losses in terms of black earning potential.

Blacks have been major economic losers in other ways as well. Because they have not possessed large land holdings, they have not been able to take advantage of governmental programs that provide subsidies for the underutilization of land; these programs are not intended to serve the poor and the struggling but the rich and secure. Blacks have also not been able to share in the enormous profits to be reaped from the relocation of industry to southern land sites. Land once owned by blacks but now in white hands is able to command many times the amount paid the original black owners. It is hard to imagine how much this factor alone has cost the black community in terms of actual cash profits.

Prevention of the further erosion of the black equity base requires extraordinary feats of success by blacks in the political process. The gains achieved through electoral politics must be expanded. It is imperative that black officials be present at every level of the federal system to protect black equity interests. Important black political units such as the Congressional Black Caucus and the Southern Conference of Black Mayors must become actively involved in the generation of legislative programs that will have a positive impact on the ability of black landowners to protect and expand their primary economic resources.

Finally, there is great need for the development of black-controlled assistance programs to give black landowners the information they need to protect and develop their land resources. The Emergency Land Fund represents a significant step forward in this respect. However, the work of this agency must be complemented by that of other key institutions. In this respect, black colleges and universities have a special responsibility. Comprehensive programs must be developed and maintained—programs that not only involve instruction in agriculture but in economics, business, accounting, psychology, history, and politics. Nothing short of a total effort by all blacks with relevant skills will be sufficient to save black land and safeguard the future of the black community.

NOTES

1. The concept of victimization has been most fully developed by St. Clair Drake, "The Social and Economic Status of the Negro in the United States," in Edward Greenberg, Neal Milner, and David J. Olson, eds., *Black Politics: The Inevitability of Conflict* (New York: Holt, Rinehart and Winston, 1971).

2. James Turner, "Blacks in the Cities: Land and Self-Determination," *The Black Scholar* (April 1970), p. 10.

3. For a discussion of black political resources, see Mathew Holden, *The Politics of the Black Nation* (New York: Chandler Publishing Company, 1973), pp. 9–16.

4. Ibid., pp. 43–52.

5. Robert S. Browne, *Only Six Million Acres: The Decline of Black Owned Land in the Rural South* (New York: The Black Economic Research Center, 1973), pp. 24–25.

6. Richard A. Cloward and Frances Fox Piven, *The Politics of Turmoil: Poverty, Race, and Urban Crisis* (New York: Vintage Books, 1965), p. 8.

7. Milton C. Fierce, "Black Struggle for Land during Reconstruction," *The Black Scholar* (February 1974), p. 14.

8. Ibid.

9. A.A. Taylor, "The Negro in the Reconstruction of Virginia," *Journal of Negro History* 11, no. 2 (April 1926), p. 374.

10. Ibid.

11. Booker T. Washington and W.E.B. Du Bois, *The Negro in the South* (Northbrook, Ill.: Metro Books, 1972), p. 105.

12. Browne, *Only Six Million Acres*, p. 19.

13. For an illuminating discussion of this disfranchisement campaign, see Steven F. Lawson, *Black Ballots* (New York: Columbia University Press, 1976), pp. 1–22.

14. Florette Henri, *Black Migration* (Garden City, N.Y.: Anchor Press, 1976), p. 21. See also J. Morgan Kousser, *Suffrage Restrictions and the Establishment of the One-Party South, 1880–1910* (New Haven: Yale University Press, 1974).

15. Harry Holloway, *The Politics of the Southern Negro* (New York: Random House, 1969), p. 21. There is evidence to suggest that this statement by Holloway sharply overstates the case. While disfranchisement sharply reduced black political strength, it did not prevent the development of an effective black leadership class and the formation of immensely influential black-controlled and operated institutions in the black community. For a careful analysis of the wide array of social, economic, and political activities taking place in southern black communities in the post-Reconstruction era, see Arnold H. Taylor, *Travail and Triumph: Black Life and Culture Since the Civil War* (Westport, Ct.: Greenwood Press, 1976).

16. A full-blown case study of black politics in Fayette County, Tennessee, can be found in Holloway, *Politics of Southern Negro*, pp. 66–90.

17. Stokely Carmichael and Charles V. Hamilton, *Black Power: The Politics of Liberation* (New York: Vintage Books, 1967), p. 133.

18. Ibid., p. 135.

19. Imari A. Obadele, "The Struggle Is for Land," *The Black Scholar* (February 1972), p. 25.

20. Imari A. Obadele, "The Struggle Is for the Republic of New Africa," *The Black Scholar* (June 1974), p. 32.

21. Browne, *Only Six Million Acres,* p. 36.

22. Anthony Griggs, "How Blacks Lost 9,000,000 Acres of Land," *Ebony* (October 1974), p. 103.

23. Charles B. Bullock III, "The Election of Blacks in the South: Pre-Conditions and Consequences" (paper presented at the 1973 annual meeting of the Southern Political Science Association, Atlanta, Ga., p. 3.

24. Ibid., p. 2.

25. Ibid., p. 3.

26. Milton Morris, *The Politics of Black America* (New York: Harper and Row, 1975), p. 156.

27. Bullock, "Election of Blacks," p. 5.

28. Ibid.

29. Ibid.

30. See Douglas St. Angelo and Paul Puryear, "The Fear and Apathy Thesis Revisited" (paper delivered at the 1976 annual meeting of the Midwest Political Science Association, Chicago, Ill.); see also U.S. Commission on Civil Rights, "Political Participation by Blacks," in Stephen J. Herzog, ed., *Minority Group Politics* (New York: Holt, Rinehart and Winston, 1971).

31. "Agricultural Schools Survive Farm Exodus," *Black Enterprise* (July 1971), pp. 26–28.

chapter 7

THE DECLINE IN BLACK-OWNED RURAL LAND: CHALLENGE TO THE HISTORICALLY BLACK INSTITUTIONS OF HIGHER EDUCATION

Carl H. Marbury

INTRODUCTION

Institutions of higher learning have three basic missions in this country: discovery of new knowledge *(research);* transfer of knowledge to others *(teaching);* and an application of that knowledge to human services *(public service).* The latter has been a special function of the unique American institution—the land-grant college/university. Until recently, black colleges including the so-called land-grant ones focused primarily on teaching, having little funds to do much of anything else.[1] The name of the game was "survival" for everything black.

The essential development of the historically black colleges was their emergence as institutions of higher education after many years as poverty-stricken primary and secondary schools. The factor that brought them into existence was the evolution and growth of a system of public education for blacks. This system, by setting up a demand for teachers, gave these colleges the preparation of teachers as their raison d'être. As a result, teacher training set in motion a complicated supply-demand chain in which the availability of teaching positions (although poorly supported by the public treasury) drew students into the colleges. These students once trained as teachers expanded the system and sent still more students to the colleges to be trained. Identifying the growth of a total system of black public education as the force responsible for the development of black colleges ascribes to these institutions a mission and an indispensable role as the source of manpower for the system and, inevitably, as the intellectual and educational control over the system; they define the content, establish methods, set the standards and are the sole outlet for the system; thus they serve as a criterion of its success.[2]

More than one hundred black colleges were founded in the United States after the Civil War to fill the needs of black men and women in a strictly segregated society. The history of their precarious but tenacious survival is among the most interesting in American higher education.

As W. E. B. Du Bois noted, if the black man was to learn, he must teach himself and take the responsibility for his own education. Southern whites refused to do much and northern whites were few and often unavailable. From sheer necessity and need there arose the historically black colleges that at first were colleges in name only, serving as elementary and secondary schools until black youth had been prepared for college-level work.[3]

In time, a number of black colleges and universities went on to win national recognition for the stature of their alumni and for academic quality. However, the very success of the black man in his struggle for justice, equality, and integration of education has increased the problems of such colleges.[4] The black population is now dispersed throughout the country and there are just as many (and maybe more) black students in historically white institutions as there are in black ones. The ratio is likely to increase and black colleges will be forced to examine and redefine their role in American higher education.

The fact of the matter is, there has never been a greater need for institutions such as the black colleges and universities than at this period in our history. The quality of life of the black masses is declining in proportion to that of other Americans and this very fact validates and sets forth a new challenge and role for black colleges and universities.

President Lyndon Johnson made a revealing and true statement at a civil rights symposium shortly before his death:

... By unconcern, by neglect, by complacent beliefs that our labors in the field of human rights are completed, we of today can seed our future with storms that would rage over the lives of our children and our children's children....

We cannot obscure this blunt fact, the black problem remains what it has always been, the simple problem of being black in a white society. That is the problem to which our efforts have not yet been addressed. To be black in a white society is not to stand on level and equal ground. While the races may stand side by side, whites stand on history's mountain and blacks stand in history's hollow. Until we overcome unequal history, we cannot overcome unequal opportunity.[5]

The wisdom and insight of President Johnson can be documented over and again. One example is that of Evelina Jenkins of Frogmore, South Carolina.[6] She is black, unlettered, and unknowing. She was forced to live the last three of her sixty-five years on the land of a cousin because her own land, the few acres where she lived most of her life, was taken away from her by an act of chicanery that is not easy to forget. The property that she originally owned was the family homestead, where her mother lived and where her grandfather farmed and reared the family.

An unscrupulous white man got Mrs. Jenkins's land. He "stole it" fair and square. For a long time she paid him $15 a year for what she thought was the tax on her property; she assumed the money was delivered by him to the tax collector's office. Then one fall when she arrived with the $15, he informed her that he owned the property and that her annual payment had not been tax money but rent. He indicated that he had owned the property for years and that he had now sold it and, therefore, she must move.

So Mrs. Jenkins moved her small house off the eight acres where she had always lived, and which she had always loved, and surrendered as well the adjoining coastal island that had also belonged to her family. The little island, wrapped in marsh grass and caressed by gentle tides, is now a middle-class white playground and residential community worth many thousands of dollars.

Mrs. Jenkins does not know how this white man came to her land. She is perplexed. Her more worldly friends surmise that he let the taxes lapse, then bought it for delinquent taxes, but she does not know and no one came to her rescue—neither the preacher nor the country agent, nor her friends or relatives.

Speaking in the lilting gullah dialect of the southern coastal islands, she told a stranger, "He didn't show me no paper. My mother, she don't know either."

Thousands of blacks in the South have lost their lands in similar fashion. Thousands more have lost theirs in less questionable ways; they have migrated to the cities and sold the land to whites or they abandoned their land altogether with the result being it was sold for delinquent taxes. Even more thousands are under pressure to sell the relatively small acreage they still own in rural areas to make way for large white-owned industries, white tourist facilities, and white residential developments.[7]

THE ROLE OF THE EMERGENCY LAND FUND (ELF)

The South's former slaves had amassed an estimated 15 million acres of land in the United States by 1910–1915. Then, when the black migration to the North began, the land began to slip away—and it has not abated since. The black community is progressively becoming a community without a land base and this has grave social, political, and economic implications for us all.[8]

Exact figures are hard to find, but estimates made from available Census Bureau statistics indicate that blacks now own no more than 5 million acres of the more than one billion agricultural acres in the nation and the decline continues at a rapid pace each year.[9]

Probably more than 4 million acres of the land owned by blacks is in the South. In South Carolina, according to census figures, blacks owned in full 5,545 farms totaling 310,373 acres in 1969. They operated an additional 169,674 acres which they partly owned and partly rented.

The situation is similar in the ten other states of the old Confederacy except for Mississippi, where in 1969 blacks still fully owned almost a million acres, more than any other state, and in Florida where, under the pressures of white immigration, they fully owned only 953 farms amounting to 78,043 acres, less than any other state.[10]

It is most ironic that it is the younger generation of blacks who have migrated from the rural southern states to the highly urbanized North and West Coast in overwhelming numbers. Many of these same young blacks who helped fashion the present black emphasis on economic goals have now belatedly come to the realization that there can be no strong economic base without a strong land base.

In the August 30, 1975, issue of the *Birmingham World* the headline was "Growing Land Loss Plagues Southern Rural Blacks." In this article Yvonne Schinhoster wrote that the problem of black-owned land loss in rural southern states is one whose implications pose a tremendous threat for the entire black community of America. The black community has historically been tied to the land. However, according to recent studies it is progressively becoming a community without a land base. If something is not done to halt the trend, "we will be completely landless by 1977," predicts Joseph L. Brooks, director of the Emergency Land Fund (ELF).[11] Since its conception several years ago, ELF has been addressing itself to the problems of the loss, acquisition, retention, and better utilization of black-owned land. Realizing the magnitude of the problem and being concerned with the fact that they may not be able to help everyone, ELF is now trying to get the federal government to recognize its responsibility.

Brooks feels that it is a governmental problem and that policies by government order should be forthcoming. Then, perhaps, the threatening trends causing black land loss could be halted. Sixty-five years ago, the black population of the United States was 9.8 million, and blacks had managed to become the full or part-time owners of more than 15 million acres of land. However, studies reveal that after 1910, the peak year for black landownership in the United States, the trend has been steadily downward. By 1969, with the national black population at 22.4 million, blacks owned only 6 million acres of land.

REASONS FOR THE DECLINE

Several reasons have been cited for the decline of black landownership: legal trickery perpetrated by southern white lawyers, land speculators, and county officials taking advantage of unsophisticated rural blacks; the rapidly emerging industrialization of the rural South; the effects of massive black migration to the urban North and West; and the general ignorance of blacks, both urban and rural, about the importance of land. We are concerned with what might be only a tiny portion of blacks, perhaps only about 25 percent of the black population. But we are also talking about what might be the root cause of the urban crisis according to Brooks who feels that the crisis was exacerbated by the great number of people coming from the country's rural areas.

According to ELF/BERC studies, although the greater portion of blacks who left rural America were probably not landowners, the migration and its cause are believed to have contributed heavily to a decline in black landownership. With the coming of the great migration, the rural percentage of the black population has been reduced to 25 percent, the southern percentage to 52 percent, and the outmigration continues virtually unabated. Recent census data show a definite reversal in this outmigration trend. Lester Salamon stresses in his explanation about black-owned land that the age bracket of most of the remaining black landowning population is significant to its decline.[12]

BLACK FARMERS AGING

More than 80 percent of the black farm-owners are over 45 years of age and close to 60 percent are over 55, according to Salamon. Therefore, there is scarcely any evidence of replenishing the ranks of black farm-owners by younger persons. The pattern appears that once the 1930s generation grows too old to farm, the land leaves black hands. All of this is taking place at a time when large stretches of land in the South are increasing in value. "Black land," says ELF director Brooks, "is tied to strategic points of development." Since the South is growing fast, it appears to be an undeveloped area. Everything is up for grabs. What is in the path of all this development is black land.

SIGNS OF CHANGE

Emergency Land Fund reports that through the formation of a growing corps of specially trained lawyers and community workers they have begun to counter the "legal" and "illegal" tricks played upon black landowners. Through the creation of new credit mechanisms, we are beginning to respond to the tremendous need for low-interest loan funds which black owners face when they attempt to develop their landholdings. Also, by working through a network of cooperative relationships with a number of rural and urban development programs, ELF is encouraging and assisting land-use programs which will transform black landholdings from economic burdens into income-yielding assets. Unsuspecting black farmers sometimes fall victim to three types of legal binds: the tax sale, the partition sale, and foreclosure. The major problem is the partition sale or heir property sale, says Brooks. This is because most blacks don't have wills; when the landowner dies the land still remains in his name, but all his heirs have an undivided interest in it. The partition sale or heir property sale is the auctioning off of a parcel of land held by several heirs of a deceased landowner. The auction usually occurs after the land has been so encumbered by legal heirs it is physically impractical or even impossible to divide it equally. Therefore, at the actual sale, most or many of the heirs are not present and a white man is usually the highest bidder and gets the land for a fraction of its market value. Emergency Land Fund's efforts in the educational and legal sense are to anticipate this problem and work to avoid it by bringing the members of a family together in order to keep the land in black hands. Also, ELF enters the actual auction process by establishing a revolving fund of cash to be used to enter fair market-price bids at partition sales. By forcing the sale price up to the market value, ELF can eliminate the enormous profitability of this vicious practice and thereby hopefully eliminate the practice itself.

DELINQUENT TAXES

In effect, the tax sale is the taking of tax-delinquent property by the state and auctioning it off to the highest bidder. This is a perfectly normal procedure, engaged in by both municipal and county governments, usually on a semiannual basis and in accordance with prescribed procedures. Yet, ELF reports that a good number of black-owned properties are lost through these sales "because the owner does not know that he owes the tax or that his property is being sold." This may occur because the owner is elderly and forgetful, because he never received a tax bill or a notice of delinquency sale, because he thought he had paid the taxes when in fact he was paying some other type of payment, or because the owner has moved away. Other cases were reported of blacks having leased their land to whites with the understanding that the tenant would pay the taxes, whereas the tenant deliberately failed to pay, concealed the tax notices, and ultimately purchased the property cheaply when it went up for auction. This was the case with Mrs. Jenkins of Frogmore, South Carolina.

Foreclosure sale property probably presents one of the more difficult techniques to counter, for in some cases the foreclosure sale is fully justified because of the willful negligence of the landowner (according to ELF). Foreclosures occur when the original owner puts up his land as collateral or security against a debt he has failed to pay, thereby relinquishing the land to his debtor. Thousands of acres of land have been lost for the price of a loan or some seed, reports Brooks. Although none of these procedures is in itself illegal, ELF investigations have revealed that a great deal of chicanery bordering on the illegal is regularly practiced by unscrupulous whites against unsuspecting or unsophisticated southern blacks. Therefore, educating the black landowner against these kinds of legal traps and other problems is an important function of the Emergency Land Fund.

CORPORATE OWNERSHIP OF AMERICA

The black community's dilemma is only part of a much larger problem that bodes nothing but misfortune for the country as a whole. Poor whites, too, have been victimized by the loss of family land. The black situation has been compounded by the much larger national picture that has tended to work against the best interests of the small and poor family farmers. Who really owns the land in this country today?[13]

One of the most disturbing factors about agricultural land in the United States is that the top twenty landowners in rural counties generally own 25 to 50 percent of the land. These owners constitute a fraction of 1 percent of the population.

Land in America is falling into fewer and fewer hands while the number of absentee landowners increases. For example, 60 percent of all the agricultural land in Iowa and Illinois is owned by absentee landowners, which is one reason why family farmers are leaving the land.

Here are some of America's major landowners and the acreage they control on a national basis. The state of New Jersey consists of 4.8 million acres, which should give one a relative idea of how land-wealthy the following corporations are:

TABLE   7.1   **Corporate Landownership**

	U.S. Acreage in millions (including some offshore)
Energy Companies	
Standard Oil of Indiana	20.3
Texaco	9.9
Mobile	7.8
Gulf	7.5

TABLE 7.1 **Continued**

Phillips Petroleum	5.3
Standard Oil of California	5.2
Continental Oil	4.5
Union Oil	4.1
Timber Companies	
International Paper	7.0
Weyerhauser	5.6
Georgia-Pacific	4.5
St. Regis	3.9
ITT	2.1
U.S. Plywood-Champion	2.0
Scott	1.8
Boise-Cascade	1.8
Union Camp	1.6
Crown-Zellerbach	1.6
Kimberly-Clark	1.5
Continental Can	1.4
Railroad Companies	
Burlington Northern	8.4
Union Pacific	7.9
Southern Pacific	5.1
St. Louis-San Francisco	1.4

Total 122.2 million acres

How can small farmers compete against and successfully resist corporate America—these super and multinational companies that are growing larger and even more powerful in the life of this nation and other countries? And how ironic that a system designed initially to foster the interests and good of common people and rural America has instead tended to exacerbate the problems of rural and urban America alike. This system is the land-grant college complex.[14]

THE LAND-GRANT COLLEGE COMPLEX: A PARADOX OF SUCCESS AND FAILURE

To understand the land-grant university system, one should read Jim

Hightower's 1972 research study, *Hard Tomatoes, Hard Times: The Failure of the Land-Grant College Complex.*[15]

This report caused some stir but it was soon ignored and seemingly forgotten. Hightower's findings were direct, simple, and somewhat frightening. He, too, seems to feel that big business and corporate agriculture's preoccupation with scientific and business efficiency has produced a radical restructuring of rural America that has been carried into urban America. According to Hightower, there has been more than a green revolution in the rural countryside in the last thirty years. There has actually been a social and economic upheaval in the American countryside. Although it is a protracted and violent revolution, it is a quiet one and is taking place with seemingly little concern about the human tragedy which is slowly evolving.

The 1862 land-grant college complex has been the scientific and intellectual father of that revolution. This public complex, established initially to serve the interests of the common man and the people of the land, has found it expedient and convenient to put its tax dollars, its facilities, its manpower, its energies, its research, and its thoughts almost solely into efforts that have worked to the advantage and profit of large corporations involved in agriculture.

The consumer is hailed as the greatest beneficiary of the land-grant college effort, but in fact consumer interests are secondary, if they are considered at all. In many cases, the complex works directly against the rural consumer including the vast majority of farmers, farm workers, and small town businessmen. Each year about a million of these people pour out of rural America into the cities. They are the waste products of an agricultural revolution designed within the 1862 land-grant college complex. Although few will admit this, today's urban crisis is a direct consequence of failure in rural America. Our technology has succeeded beyond our wildest dreams. Of course, the entire blame for that failure cannot be placed on the land-grant complex, but no single institution, private or public, has played a more crucial role in the human disaster incurred.

The complex has been eager to work with farm machinery manufacturers and well-capitalized farming operations to mechanize all agricultural labor, but it has accepted no responsibility for the farm laborer who is put out of work by technology. It has worked hand in hand with seed companies to develop high-yield seed strains, but it has not noticed that rural America is yielding up practically all of its young people. It has been available day and night to help nonfarming corporations develop schemes of vertical integration, while offering independent family farmers little more comfort than "adapt or die." It has devoted hours to the creation of adequate water systems for fruit and vegetable processors and canners, but many rural communities still have no central water systems. It has tampered with the gene structure of tomatoes, strawberries, asparagus, and other foods to prepare them for the steel grasp of mechanical harvesters, but it has sat still while the American food supply has been laced with carcinogenic and chemical substances which are gradually shortening the lives of many Americans—black and white.

THE MORRILL ACTS

The Morrill Act passed by Congress and signed by President Lincoln in 1862 is justly celebrated as the most important single piece of federal legislation affecting higher education in the nineteenth century; it established the basis for the land-grant institutions that developed throughout the country, most successfully perhaps in the states of the Middle West.[16] Less well known is the Morrill Act of 1890, the so-called Second Morrill Act, which made possible the establishment of separate black land-grant colleges in southern and border states. The history of these colleges is perhaps the most blatant and devastating case of discrimination relating to the dual system of higher education perpetrated by federal and state governments.[17]

The Second Morrill Act was not passed specifically for black higher education but to obtain more operating money for the 1862 colleges. The 1890 act happened to include a "separate but equal" provision authorizing the establishment of colleges for blacks.[18] Having done this, Congress left the institutions to the states, the result being a despicable history of deprivation of funding. Black colleges were not allowed to become partners in any sense of the word in the land-grant complex. Resource allocations were blatantly discriminatory from the very beginning. In 1971, of the $76,800,000 in USDA funds allocated to those sixteen states with both white and black land-grant colleges, 99.5 percent went to the white colleges leaving only .5 percent for black colleges.[19] Less than 1 percent of the research money distributed by the

Cooperative State Research Service in 1971 went to black land-grant colleges.[20] Hightower's observation was right on target when he said:

> The solution to the problems of rural America is not a return to the land plow. Rather, land-grant colleges' researchers must get out of the comfortable chairs of corporate board rooms and get back to serving the independent producer and the common man of rural America. It means returning to the historic mission of taking the technological revolution to all who need it, rather than smugly assuming that they will be able to keep pace. Instead of adopting the morally bankrupt posture that millions of people must inevitably be squeezed out of agriculture and out of rural America, land grant colleges must turn their thoughts, energies and resources to the task of keeping people on the farm, in the small town and out of cities. It means turning from the erroneous assumption that big is good, that what serves Ralston Purina serves rural America. It means research for the consumer rather than for the processor. In short, it means putting the research focus on people first—not as a trickle-down after thought.[21]

THE CHALLENGE AND UNIQUE OPPORTUNITY OF THE BLACK LAND-GRANT COLLEGE

This emerging tragedy which touches all Americans and the disturbing tragedy of the continuous loss of a black community land base constitutes an urgent challenge for the historically black institutions of higher education, especially for the sixteen black land-grant colleges. These institutions should and must take the lead in arresting and redressing a bad situation. They are in the best position of all to act in accordance with the raison d'être of land-grant colleges—that is, to help the poor and the general populace of America's rural countryside.[22]

Tennessee Tombigbee Waterway Project is a multibillion-dollar federal works project designed to link the Tombigbee and Tennessee rivers. The waterway will provide a new inland water route to connect the Port of Mobile with Nashville, the Midwest, and Chicago. Once fully developed for navigation, the waterway will yield increased industrial and agribusiness growth in southwest Alabama and northwest Mississippi.[23]

These two state areas have large and highly concentrated black populations. In fact, at least 40 percent of the population in the area is black. And yet, the TTWDA and other planning agencies with responsibility for the waterway have little or token black participation and representation on their boards of directors and in their membership. A major rationale for the project is its anticipated benefits in increasing economic growth and employment opportunities for low-income people in the area.

On January 19, 1974, the Federation of Southern Cooperatives and its member state association in Alabama and Mississippi convened the First Peoples' Conference on the Tennessee-Tombigbee Waterway. It was held at Epes, Alabama. Approximately two hundred persons were in attendance. As an outgrowth of this first conference the Minority Peoples' Council on the Tennessee-Tombigbee Waterway was organized. The council was conceived as a continuing committee to pursue the issues and concerns raised at the conference for full participation in all aspects of the construction, operation, and development of the waterway. Among its several objectives are three (discussed later in this chapter) which have important implications for black land-grant colleges: who else is in the best position to try and redress the rural-urban imbalance? Perhaps the other big land-grant colleges will eventually wake up to what they have wrought but this cannot be assumed because of the peculiar nature of the vicious cycle they helped engender and of which they are a constituent part.[24]

The black land-grant college is in an enviable position to serve the real interests of black and white poor people in each of the several states. By doing so and by expending their funds and resources in the all-important area of human resources research and development, black land-grant colleges would do much to insure their continued existence as well as preserve themselves for the uphill struggle ahead as we move closer toward the year 2000. In the long run, only the people can assure the long-range future of black colleges. The people are unlikely to insist on the continued existence of those colleges and/or universities who choose to ignore the problems, concerns, and interests of the masses of black people in a given state; what black college can afford to ignore this problem of problems—the loss of precious land? The time has come for black land-grant colleges to rise to the occasion and some of them are doing just that. They will never again have this opportunity to lead in quite this fashion because the land once lost cannot be regained.

BLACK LAND-GRANT COLLEGES AND THE TENNESSEE-TOMBIGBEE WATERWAY PROJECT

Another challenge to black land-grant colleges, especially those located in Alabama, Mississippi, Tennessee, Kentucky, and Florida, is some form of active involvement in the massive Tennessee-Tombigbee Waterway Project (TTWP).[25] Three areas, as defined by the Minority Peoples' Council, lend themselves to these institutions' participation:

1. *Minority Land Ownership:* to identify, maintain, and protect the landholdings of black people in the impact area of the TTW; to assist black people in developing their landholdings in agricultural, industrial, and recreational enterprises, in relation to the waterway.

2. *Educational Institutions:* to recognize the unique role of black institutions of higher learning in relation to the TTW[26]; to encourage and assist these institutions, in the impact area of the waterway, to develop curricula and programs to prepare their students and their community for involvement and employment on the waterway.

3. *Research:* to develop and engage in a research program to bring all the pertinent facts and information on the TTW to the attention of the minority community for their awareness, discussion, and action. Research will be done in conjunction with educational institutions and other concerned organizations in the area.

The Tennessee-Tombigbee Waterway Project is the chance of a lifetime for black land-grant colleges to help raise the standard of living and improve the quality of life of thousands of black families. Will the job be done collectively as land-grant colleges? Will the job be done cooperatively with other organizations who are busy fostering the interests of the black poor; or will we be content to have business and education remain separate as usual?

CREATIVE PARTNERSHIPS AND UNITED EFFORTS

The TTWP is an opportunity for black land-grant colleges to develop "people-centered" outreach creative alliances and fruitful partnerships with certain agencies which have proven track records regarding the impoverished masses.[27] The colleges should take several initiatives immediately:

First, each black land-grant college in the sixteen states should expend some of its recently acquired USDA funds addressing the critical problem of black land loss within each state.

Second, as many land-grant colleges as possible should get together so as to coordinate and harness their collective resources in an intensive and broad-based effort to reverse the spiraling loss of land still taking place within the black community.

Third, the colleges should initiate a cooperative program with the Emergency Land Fund taking full advantage of those groups which already have had years of experience working on this problem.

Fourth, the colleges should learn about and make their resources available to the Federation of Southern Cooperatives which is headquartered in the heart of the TTWP area.

Fifth, each college should establish a permanent interdepartmental task force on the TTWP to sponsor seminars to foster research and to explore the educational, academic, and long-range vocational/placement implications of this project.

IMAGINATION AND INNOVATION FOR QUALITY OF LIFE

It is a time for collective innovation within the total black community—innovation which is immediate, widespread, and long-range. This innovation must be imaginative, grass roots, and down-to-earth—based upon the very best thinking, planning, and action. The existential alienation and "madness" of life is likely to wreak great havoc upon the black American community unless some well-thought-out and innovative efforts are made by black people themselves to head off the crisis before it gets too far out of hand.[28] In realistic terms, black people are facing a "quality of life" crisis of infinite proportions as we move toward the year 2000.

The necessity for renewed leadership and undiminished effort is indicated in a 1976 report, "The State of Black America," by the National Urban League.[29] Citing both the national economy and loss of national commitment, the league says that many past gains for blacks were erased or "badly eroded" during 1975. Acknowledging individual exceptions to the trend, the report emphasized "the growing number of black income, new public displays of racism, and the negative attitude of policymakers toward programs that aid the poor." Today, black colleges and universities have a mission and purpose as great and as important as any other American institution of higher education. Their work is cut out for them.

Dr. G. M. Sawyer, president of Texas Southern University, has summed up the challenge:

> Somehow, it must be made clear that the forces of community life are quite impersonal and their negative effects will alter the quality of life for everyone. Similarly, we must know that every item, every person, every institution in the community has its place or its moment of usefulness to the short-range and the long-range goals of that community. Those of us who lay claim to leadership in these times must use all of our wisdom to see that the dynamics of the ingredients of the community interface for our common good.[30]

NOTES

1. Notable exceptions have been such institutions as Howard University (Law and Civil Rights), Fisk and Atlanta University (Social Sciences), and Tuskegee Institute (Agricultural Sciences and Extension Service). Many other colleges and normal schools offered limited community service within their immediate locales.

2. See F. Bowles and F. A. DeCosta, *Between Two Worlds: A Profile of Negro Higher Education* (New York: McGraw-Hill, 1971). See also D. O. W. Holmes, *The Evolution of the Negro College* (New York: Columbia University Press, 1934), and E. J. McGrath, *The Predominantly Negro Colleges and Universities in Transition* (New York: Columbia University Press, 1965).

3. Du Bois cites the fact that in a single generation black colleges put 30,000 black teachers in the South; they wiped out the illiteracy of the majority of the black people of the land, and they made Tuskegee possible.

4. Ironically, there is a *legal* threat to black public higher education. In the fall of 1970 a team of attorneys for the NAACP Legal Defense Fund and the Washington law firm of Rauh and Silard decided to take the federal government to court. They asked a district judge in Washington, Judge John H. Pratt, to make the U.S. Department of Health, Education, and Welfare stop providing funds to public schools and colleges still practicing racial discrimination. The case became known as Adams v. Richardson—Adams being John Quincy Adams, a black Mississippian and father of six children whose name appeared first in an alphabetical listing of the plaintiff, and Richardson being Elliot L. Richardson, who at the time was secretary of HEW. The plaintiff's basic argument in Adams v. Richardson was direct and simple. Title VI of the Civil Rights

Act of 1964 declares that all forms of racial discrimination are prohibited in programs receiving federal financial assistance, and it requires federal agencies providing such assistance to cut off the funds if the recipients fail to comply with the law. The attorneys for the plaintiff proved to Judge Pratt's satisfaction that HEW was not enforcing Title VI (he was later upheld by the U.S. Court of Appeals for the District of Columbia) and so he ordered ten states (Arkansas, Georgia, Florida, Maryland, Mississippi, Louisiana, North Carolina, Oklahoma, Pennsylvania, and Virginia) to produce comprehensive plans for desegregating their colleges and universities. The litigation and negotiations have continued since that time and in 1977 Judge Pratt ruled (and HEW concurred) that this desegration must proceed but *not at the expense of the historically black institutions*.

5. Quoted in H. Howe II, "Black Colleges and the Continuing Dream," a Ford Foundation reprint of remarks by Dr. Howe, vice president for education and research, the Ford Foundation, at the inauguration of Samuel DuBois Cook as president of Dillard University, New Orleans, April 3, 1976.

6. "Blacks Struggle to Keep Little Land They Have Left," *New York Times*, December 7, 1972, p. 39.

7. See Robert S. Browne, *Only Six Million Acres: A Decline of Black Owned Land in the Rural South* (New York: The Black Economic Research Center, 1973).

8. See Leo McGee and Robert Boone, *Black Rural Land Ownership: A Matter of Economic Survival* (Nashville: Tennessee State University Press, 1976).

9. The Emergency Land Fund Office and Dr. Lester M. Salamon at Duke University estimate that blacks are losing land at the rate of 333,000 acres a year. In 1915, 9.8 million blacks owned approximately 15 million acres. In 1969, 22.4 million blacks owned only 6 million acres of land.

10. Eleven southern states comprise the basis for the rural black land in America. They are Alabama, Arkansas, Florida, Georgia, Louisiana, Mississippi, North Carolina, South Carolina, Tennessee, Texas, and Virginia.

11. See Joseph F. Brooks, *The Emergency Land Fund: A Five Year Report, 1972–1977* (Atlanta, Ga.: Emergency Land Fund, 1977).

12. Lester Salamon, "Profile of a Disappearing Equity Base: Trends and Economic Characteristics of Black-owned Land" (Durham, N.C.: Duke University Institute of Policy Sciences, 1972).

13. *Parade Sunday Magazine,* June 8, 1975, p. 10.

14. The land-grant complex is made up of three interrelated units, all of which are attached to the land-grant college campuses. The first unit is comprised of the Colleges of Agriculture created in 1862 by the Morrill Act. The State Agricultural Experiment Stations are the second unit. They were created in 1887 by the Hatch Act for the purpose of conducting agricultural and rural

research in cooperation with the colleges of agriculture. The Extension Service, created in 1914 by the Smith-Lever Act, is the third unit. It was designed to bring the fruits of research to all rural people.

15. The Agribusiness Accountability Project, a public-interest research and advocacy organization based in Washington, D.C., created the Task Force on the Land Grant Complex to examine this issue and to publish its findings. In addition to research done in Washington and by correspondence, studies were carried out on the campuses of several state universities—California, Cornell, Florida, Iowa State, Maryland, Michigan State, North Carolina State, Purdue, and Texas A & M.

16. The Morrill Act of 1862 was the first federal aid of any kind to higher education in this country. This aid was provided through gifts of land to each state to endow a public college but no provision was made regarding those states where the black population was in slavery.

17. The second act sanctioned the establishment of second land-grant colleges in states which wanted them. Seventeen states eventually chose to do this (several states were very slow in doing so) by designating existing private black schools as the second land-grant institution, by designating existing state-supported black institutions, by assigning the meager funds to existing private black schools and subsequently taking them over as state institutions, or by establishing new land-grant colleges for blacks under state control. Alcorn A & M, now Alcorn State University, became the first of the seventeen when so designated in 1878.

18. The Act reads ". . . the establishment and maintenance of such colleges separately for white and colored students will be held to be in compliance with the provisions of this act if the funds received in such State or Territory be equitably divided as hereinafter set forth" (U.S. Department of the Interior, 1894, vol. I, p. 620).

19. West Virginia discontinued the separate black land-grant status of West Virginia State in 1957. Three others, however, in Arkansas, Maryland, and Texas have been absorbed into the respective state systems.

20. It was not until 1972, after several years of hard work and tenacious persistence, that the efforts of Dr. Richard D. Morrison, president of Alabama A & M University, and other black land-grant college presidents began to pay off in significant ways. For over eighty years the colleges received only meager fundings as a result of their land-grant status. Then in 1972, under the leadership and through the support of Secretary Hardin, the USDA appropriated $14 (and later $17) million for *extension* and *research* at black land-grant colleges, including Tuskegee Institute. (See the *OAPNC Newsletter,* Atlanta, Ga, December 1975.) More recently, Dr. Morrison and a task force of black land-grant presidents succeeded in getting congressional action on a legislative act which should make possible permanent funding for expanded programs at black land-

grant colleges. This *Food and Agriculture Act of 1977* is a major milestone as well as a great opportunity for these colleges and universities.

21. See *Society Magazine,* November/December 1972, p. 22, an excerpted section from Jim Hightower.

22. The poor have progressively gotten short shrift from the 1862 institutions. For a long time, they did benefit from the Extension Service, but in recent years since the demise of the small farmer, Extension has been preoccupied with efficiency and production—a focus that has contributed much to the largest producers. And, while the rural poor get little attention from ES professionals, they receive band-aid assistance from highly visible but marginally helpful programs. In 1955, a Special Needs Section was added to Extension legislation, setting aside a sum of money to assist disadvantaged areas, but Extension was slow to make use of it. Now for the first time, black land-grant colleges are using their Extension funds primarily to help poor people—both black and white.

23. Construction of the 253-mile water route is scheduled to last a full decade (1973– 1983). Construction of the initial two locks and dams was initiated at Gainesville and Aliceville, Ala. The project is supervised by the U.S. Army Corps of Engineers, but eventual control of the waterway is vested in the Tennessee-Tombigbee Waterway Development Authority (TTWDA), a five-state group with membership appointed by the governors of Alabama, Mississippi, Florida, Kentucky, and Tennessee.

24. Hightower indicates that land-grant policy is the product of closed community with very definite vested interests. The administrators, academics, and scientists, along with USDA officials and corporate executives, have locked themselves into an inbred and even incestuous complex, and they are incapable of thinking beyond their self-interest and traditional concepts of agricultural re search.

25. The information on TTWP comes from two sources: (a) *People's Guide to Tennessee-Tombigbee Waterway* printed by the Cooperator Press: Federation of Southern Cooperatives Rural Training and Research Center, Epes, Ala., copyright © applied for 1975; and (b) from an article by Thomas A. Johnson, in the *New York Times,* October 12, 1976, p. 18.

26. In December 1975, the Alabama Center for Higher Education under the leadership of Dr. Richard Arrington, Jr., Executive Director, began a cooperative working relationship with the Federation of Southern Cooperatives. Through its recently funded Human Resources Research and Development Program (conceived initially by Dr. Arrington, Rev. V. Castle Stewart, and this author), ACHE could now reach out and lend a hand to a black agency serving a constituency of 30,000 rural low-income families.

27. Robert S. Browne, executive director of the black Economic Research Center in New York, has made a strong case for a mission such as this by black

land-grant colleges in his paper prepared for the Southern Rural Task Force (May 1975), *The Role of Land in the Development of Southern Rural Black Communities* (see pages 25ff.). Tennessee State University has pioneered in this regard through the work of Dr. Leo McGee and Robert Boone. TSU was the first black land-grant college to receive CSRS/USDA funds specifically for the study of rural landownership, control problems, and attitudes of minorities toward land within the state as a whole. The title of the McGee-Boone research project report is *A Study of Rural Landownership, Control Problems and Attitudes of Blacks toward Rural Land,* published under the auspices of the Tennessee State University Extension and Continuing Education Program.

28. Orlando Patterson, ''The Moral Crisis of the Black American,'' *The Public Interest* (Summer 1973), pp. 43–69.

29. See *The State of Black America,* issued by the National Urban League, January 28, 1976.

30. G. M. Sawyer, ''Black Colleges and Development,'' *Journal of Black Studies* 6, no. 1, September 1975.

chapter 8

THE EMERGENCY LAND FUND: A RURAL LAND RETENTION AND DEVELOPMENT MODEL

Joseph Brooks

INTRODUCTION

The Southeast is often referred to as a New Frontier for economic development and expansion. This label, whether justified or not, is catching on and is echoed by individuals and institutions in both the public and private sectors, by foreign investment groups, and, understandably, by politicians in an election year that may produce a southern president.

Areas of the rural Southeast which were underdeveloped and isolated as recently as ten to fifteen years ago are in 1979 new towns and resort developments; they encompass the present or planned routes of new highway and water transportation systems, of new oil and gas fields, and of nuclear power generators; they are producers of a growing share of the nation's and the world's food and fiber needs. In short, they clearly exhibit the beginnings of potentially tremendous industrial and commercial developments. In the face of such dramatic change, the Emergency Land Fund (ELF) raises the question: *With more than 50 percent of the total United States black population residing in fourteen southern states, and with half that number being rural, how and through what means will blacks benefit from this growing prosperity of the South?*

This chapter will concern itself with the activities of ELF in addressing the opportunities and the problems of the inclusion of blacks in the expanding prosperity of the rural Southeast region. The particular focus of the ELF program is the extent to which these opportunities are in-

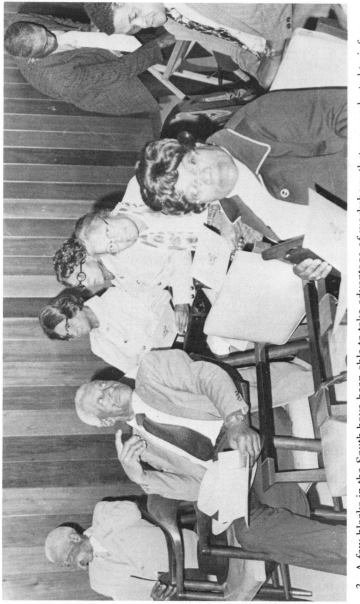

3. A few blacks in the South have been able to take advantage of workshops that are conducted to inform them of the legal aspects concerning rural landownership. *Photo by John Cross*

creasingly being diminished through the loss of black-owned land and the attendant outmigration of blacks from the South.

THE BLACK LAND LOSS PROBLEM

It is a well-documented fact that America's population has become increasingly urban, although there are some signs that this urbanization process is slowing. In 1870, the United States was only 2.5 percent urban while in 1970 an estimated 75 percent of all Americans resided in urban areas. It has been further projected that by the year 2000 the United States will be 85 percent urban. Although the urbanization trend has been evident among all ethnic segments of the population, the rate of urbanization has been especially high in the black community.

A primary pull factor for outmigration generally has been the promise of higher wages and a better standard of living offered by urban areas. This was clearly the case during World Wars I and II when the United States' war effort, and consequently the northern industries, needed a larger labor pool. Since the mid-1950s, however, the absorptive capacity of the urban centers (New York City is a prime example), especially as regards untrained and unskilled labor, has declined noticeably and with it the relative attractiveness of urban migration. Nevertheless, migration to urban areas, albeit on a reduced scale, has continued, in large part due to the bleak economic picture for rural people; this is particularly true for the black rural family. For example, in 1965, during a relatively healthy economic period, 68 percent of nonwhite farm families were below the poverty level and 56 percent of nonwhite, nonfarm families living in small towns and rural areas were below the poverty level. The picture a decade later is not likely to reveal significant change.

The Emergency Land Fund has set for itself the task of helping to improve the economic conditions of the southern black landowner by focusing on his land, which is usually his major capital asset. Research on black landownership has revealed that the land base for blacks was at its maximum in 1910, when blacks owned some 15 million acres. By 1950, this figure had declined to 12.5 million, and since that time the acceleration has been astounding with the most recent Census of Agriculture (1969) placing the figure at something less than 6 million acres.[1] This recent decline in black landownership has coincided with the migration of blacks from the rural South as well as with the rise in southern land values and the emergence of the new, industrializing southern frontier. If blacks are to benefit from these contemporary trends in the southern economy, it is clear that their past patterns of outmigration and separation from their land must be reversed.

The ELF program operates on the assumption that one means of reversing this trend is by helping blacks who own land to bring that land into profitable production. In this way the landowner can be provided an income which will presumably eliminate his need either to migrate or to dispose of his land.

The heart of the ELF program during most of its eight years of existence has been focused simply on helping blacks retain title to their land in the face of a broad range of barely legal and clearly illegal practices which have long been used to deprive them of their holdings. Closely related to these "courthouse"-type problems, which stem largely from landowners being black or being uneducated, are a host of different problems which arise from the landowner being poor. These are the cases where land is being foreclosed because the owner actually cannot meet his payments. Often in such cases the key to retaining the land is simply to find some means of making it sufficiently productive to yield a positive return. In the past year, ELF has given increased attention to this latter problem of land development. Land retention and land development thus constitute the dual thrust of the Emergency Land Fund program.

THE EMERGENCY LAND FUND PROGRAM

When ELF began operations it had no model to follow and possessed precious little detailed information about the real problems which were resulting in the astonishing loss of land by southern rural blacks. Because there was no place to turn for guidance, ELF used trial-and-error techniques to learn what the real problems were and what methods would be most effective in addressing them. Since there were no experienced persons in the field, ELF staffed itself with concerned and committed individuals, described the problems, and then the staff trained itself. This was true even with black lawyers. They had to be alerted to the problems, for rural real estate law was generally well outside their experience.

During its first three years ELF launched a major attack on the three practices which were so frequently found to be the basis for so much of the black land loss: the tax sale, the partition sale, and the foreclosure. All three are, of course, legal in and of themselves. The problem is that they are so frequently utilized in abusive, discriminatory, and marginally legal ways.

TAX SALES, PARTITION SALES, FORECLOSURES

In the tax sale, for example, a landowner's failure to pay his taxes for two or three consecutive years can lead to the ultimate loss of his land. Furthermore, anyone may pay these taxes and thereby gain a legal hold on the land. Procedures for notifying landowners when their taxes are due are often lax—sometimes purposely so when it comes to blacks— and vast amounts of black-owned land have been unintentionally lost via this tactic.

The partition sale is, if anything, a more vicious instrument than the tax sale. Under this practice, property owned by a number of heirs (so called heir property) may be brought to a forced sale (to transform the land value into cash so that it may be partitioned among the heirs) by anyone who obtains an heir's interest, whether by purchase or otherwise, no matter how small. Once such a sale is demanded, there is typically no bidder other than the individual forcing the sale (the people living on the land are usually too poor to bid, and the court requires cash) so the land is likely to be sold for a fraction of its true value as the owners watch helplessly. Because heir property is very common among rural blacks owing to superstitions about the making of wills, the black community is particularly vulnerable to the unscrupulous partition sale brought about by someone buying out the interest of a single heir and then demanding that the land be sold.

Foreclosures, the third practice through which much black-owned land is lost, although commonplace, are less often the result of overt chicanery than of economic hardship. Regardless of their motivation, however, they are a major cause of blacks losing their land and consequently must be addressed as a problem. Was the loan reasonable and valid in the first place? Why can't the mortgagee meet the payments? These and other questions must be examined in determining the true source of the problem and in planning how to overcome it.

During ELF's early period when it was first learning about and experimenting with ways to thwart these practices, it enjoyed some of its most gratifying moments. Although these nefarious tax sales had probably been taking place for nearly a century, ELF staff found itself to be the only blacks in attendance. The first time ELF staff appeared at such sales the atmosphere immediately became tense, the consternation palpable. Needless to say, ELF representatives were also uneasy at these early encounters, but this situation has so fully reversed itself that today the local black people are beginning to come to the tax sales themselves, demanding to see the tax record books, and otherwise exercising rights which they had been intimidated from exercising in the past. An ELF staffer, attending his first tax sale in one Mississippi county, reported overhearing one white official remarking to another that not only were niggers present but that he had heard from someone at the bank that the niggers had "just deposited a big check from up in New York."

Whites are getting used to seeing blacks at the tax sales now, and hopefully the blatant abuses are being corrected. The appearance of an ELF team at a partition sale, however, continues to provoke the consternation of the manipulators who think they are going to walk off with a poor black family's property by paying only a fraction of its true value. When they discover that their bidding will not go unopposed the frustration becomes evident; ELF usually comes to such sales prepared to bid up to the true market value. Fortunately, the bidding rarely goes this high; ELF wins the bid and becomes owner of the land. The heir interest which forced the sale of the land is paid off and ELF resells the land to the family at the bid price plus expenses. An unscrupulous plot has been thwarted, the family is able to remain on its land, and hopefully the perpetrators are discouraged from continuing this nefarious practice.

Since participation in partition sales ties up substantial sums of money, ELF is able to respond to only a portion of those which come to its attention. It is convinced, however, that its involvement in such sales is already having a chilling effect on this practice and, like the tax sales, consider this program as one of its real success areas in which it identified a problem which no one had ever before addressed, explored how best to attack it, and then proceeded to implement an effective program.

EMERGENCY LOAN FUND

The ELF learned very early that lack of money and of access to money was a major cause of black land loss. Like most small farmers, black farmers operate on the bare edge of solvency much of the time. Bad weather, a poor crop, a major illness of the key member of the household, can quickly push the family into insolvency. In addition, farmers generally have to borrow money to get their crops into the ground, and sometimes to get their crops out of the ground and to the market as well.

In the rural South, obtaining such capital funds has always been a problem for blacks. Racial prejudice and institutionalized racism have converged with the frail economic and educational base of many black families to earn the black farmer a place at the tail end of the credit line. Without credit, few farmers are able to operate. Yet the black southern farmer has faced a history of refusal of credit, or of obtaining it only on the most onerous of terms, terms which are strictly enforced at the least sign of noncompliance. The staff quickly discovered that if it was to go about the business of saving land, it clearly needed a loan fund.

Approximately $200,000 was earmarked by ELF for this purpose—an amount which was rather quickly exhausted and which needed to be many times greater. As a revolving fund making mainly short-term loans, however, it has been able to lend out considerably more than the $200,000 over a period of several years. Unfortunately, ELF's sharply

TABLE 8.1   **Emergency Loan Fund Analysis**

Fifty-seven (57) loans over a three-and-one-half year period ending August 31, 1976.

	Dollars	*Percent*
Total loans during period	− $272,388.10	100.
Dollar amount paid back	− 112,770.35	41.4
Loss or uncollectable loans	− 1,298.00	.47
Schedule of Loans Outstanding		
Past Due	$ 28,679.63	10.5
Due by 8/31/77	83,797.51	30.7
Due by 8/31/78	21,026.90	7.7
Due by 8/31/79	10,923.49	4.0
Due by 8/31/80	8,136.16	2.9
Due by 8/31/81	2,424.91	1.0
Due by 8/31/82	1,786.17	.7
Due by 8/31/83	1,138.28	.4
Due by 8/31/84	406.70	.1

Average size of loan is $4,780 with interest rates varying between 4.5 and 5 percent.

reduced fund availabilities during the year 1976 have resulted in its having to use loan repayments for operating expenses; the fund began to dwindle and will eventually extinguish itself unless replenished.

The ELF's experience with its loan fund has been highly encouraging. Table 8.1 indicates that its loss ratio has been remarkably low—less than 5 percent. Even if one adds the past-due loans, the figure rises to only 11 percent. This compares favorably with many financial institutions making this type of loan.

In practice, the loan program has not only enabled ELF to save land directly, it has also provided ELF a means to get close enough to the farmers to permit an analysis of their situations and in many cases provide them with the direction and technical assistance they need if they are to avoid future insolvencies. The importance of having cash available to put up when it is needed cannot be overestimated in terms of being an effective means for prodding conservative landowners to take the necessary steps to tighten up their operations or to instigate whatever changes may be required to increase their chances of success.

THE LUBA PROJECT

Most black rural landowners have small holdings, ranging from one to 50 acres. A high portion, possibly the majority of these plots, are not being put to any productive use. Although many are undoubtedly idle because the owner is absent, many more are not worked because the owners feel that it is no longer profitable to cultivate them. Frequently, cotton is the only crop which these landowners have had experience in cultivating and with current cotton prices it is indeed no longer profitable to grow the crop on small acreages and with hand labor.

There are, however, other crops which can be profitably grown on these small acreages; in fact, some can even be grown by a family whose main breadwinner works at a full-time job elsewhere. With the average family income in these areas often as low as $2,000 a year, social and economic payoff from an effective utilization of the land is self-evident. What is needed is for the farmer to be made aware of the possibilities, to be provided the necessary technical information and management skills, and to be directed toward operating capital and market outlets.

In an effort to meet some of these needs, ELF has launched a project which it calls Land Utilization Benefiting Agriculture (LUBA). This

project recognizes the needs of these small landowners and it also recognizes that the land-grant colleges' government-funded extension service programs, designed to assist the farm population, are failing to
meet the needs of such farmers. The emphasis at the agriculture experiment stations has been on agribusiness and on a technology which is not
available or suitable to the small black farmer. The County Extension
agents, whose task is to popularize the newer agricultural discoveries
and techniques among the farm population, are themselves handicapped
by the inappropriateness of much of their information.[2] There have also
been racial and other barriers which have prevented black landowners
from benefiting from the government-funded Extension work. The
LUBA project is intended to help fill this void and to convert idle land
into a productive asset for many poor black landowners.

During its first year (1975–1976) the LUBA project undertook two
major efforts:

1. To organize a group of farmers to grow specific crops for markets
   which ELF had located.
2. To demonstrate to farmers in the project area the feasibility of
   profitably growing greenhouse tomatoes.

The overall results of this effort are quite encouraging, especially
as regards the production and marketing of crops on small acreages.
Cucumbers and Irish potatoes were successfully marketed and yielded a
favorable return. Although the demonstration farm was less successful,
the LUBA staff, which previously knew nothing about raising
greenhouse tomatoes, feels confident that they have learned enough to
carry through a successful demonstration this year; the problems they
encountered will better equip them to warn the farmers of pitfalls.

CHALLENGE TO THE FARMERS HOME ADMINISTRATION (FmHA)

The FmHA emerged as an operating agency of the U.S. Department
of Agriculture in the early 1900s for the purpose of providing finance
capital and other services to small landowners. It grew out of the so-
cially oriented FDR New Deal Farms Security Administration of the late
1930s. However, FmHA today no longer resembles the congressional
mandate given it and ELF maintains that this departure has been at the
expense of rural blacks.

For the past two years ELF has intervened on behalf of black landowners seeking acquisition or operating capital, as well as to convince FmHA in some cases not to foreclose on certain loans. These efforts have carried ELF to the top of the FmHA structure where it has argued, with documentation, the unclear and sometimes arbitrary criteria applied to blacks seeking acquisition and operating capital loans.

In June 1975, ELF staff met with national and state representatives of FmHA in Montgomery, Alabama, to discuss several cases that ELF had documented suggesting unclear and arbitrary policies of the agency as they relate to blacks. At the meeting ELF presented a thirteen-page document, "Federal Financing for Black Rural Development: A Report Focusing on FmHA Credit Barriers for Minorities in Eleven Southern States."

One area of documented abuse presented at the Montgomery meeting was the concern for farm ownership loans. These loans are a critical resource to the survival of small and medium-size agricultural operations in the South. The ELF research shows that blacks have consistently been restricted in both the number and amount of farm ownership loans received from FmHA. A specific example was noted in Mississippi. With blacks representing 42 percent of the farm population in 1974, they received only 8 percent of the state's farm ownership money. Further, the average size of a loan to whites was $27,000 in 1974 as compared to only $14,000 for blacks. Research shows that this pattern closely resembles disparities in ten other southern states.

The following factors are considered impediments to the full participation of blacks in the FmHA:
1. Lack of community training and information about FmHA programs.
2. Relegation of FmHA black employees to nondecision-making positions.
3. Excessive loan processing periods, culuminating in the loss of black-owned land and increased debt.
4. Biased exercise of discretionary powers in extending credit to and imposing foreclosure on black borrowers.
5. Credit denial to moderate-income blacks with limited risk capability statements.
6. Underextension of emergency, ownership, recreation, and water and soil loans to blacks, particularly in those counties where blacks comprise 30 percent or more of the population (rural redlining).

The ELF proposes to address the situation indirectly through efforts to:

1. Put minority institutions and organizations in a position to package opportunities for black rural residents.
2. Increase pressure upon Washington FmHA administrators to develop compliance procedures that will ensure equal opportunity and affirmative action in county FmHA offices.
3. Provide members of Congress and nonfederal elected black officials with documented insight into the problems of black people on the land.
4. Enlist the support and involvement of elected black officials in monitoring and overseeing FmHA activities and the Department of Agriculture's minority record in the South.
5. Aid policymakers in the development of legislative mechanisms that will align FmHA program implementation with Congress's intent that this agency serve the needs of all the people and in particular the black southern rural farm population.

COUNTY CONTACT SYSTEM

By 1974, ELF felt that it had acquired sufficient familiarity with enough key aspects of land-retention techniques to allow it to begin to train the community to monitor its own land problems. The work which was done in a score of counties needed to be multiplied many times over if the problems were to be addressed on a southwide scale, and clearly the best way to expand the program was through a community organizing process.

Thus was launched a system of County Contacts, initially in 44 counties in Mississippi and subsequently extended to 17 counties in Alabama. At present, the County Contact System (CCS) operates in 61 of the 149 counties comprising the states of Mississippi and Alabama.

The participants in the CCS are volunteer workers located in 61 CCS counties. After an orientation session provided by ELF field staff, the County Contacts take on the responsibility of identifying and informing the ELF state office of the land-related problems affecting black residents in their respective communities. One vital source of information is the legal notices section of the newspaper, where tax and partition sales are generally listed (rural blacks rarely read such items). Blacks whose land is being put up for tax or partition sale are alerted by the County

Contact. If some of them cannot be located or are unable to avert the sale, the County Contact notifies the ELF state office and ELF staff attempts to provide the needed assistance.

County Contacts do, on behalf of ELF and their communities, participate in the bidding process at tax and partition sales. Also, some volunteers have learned to conduct title searches, to collect and disseminate information, and to perform other vital functions that have proved to be essential to the overall operation of ELF and highly useful to their own communities. Land Education workshops are frequently held throughout the CCS counties and training sessions or the County Contacts are provided by the ELF field staff. Additionally, there is a competition among the County Contacts, wherein the person responsible for saving the most land during a given period is awarded a prize. The prizes are United States savings bonds, awarded on a quarterly and yearly basis.

The scope of the County Contacts' activity expands as the ELF program expands. In Mississippi, where ELF's demonstration farm is under way, it is expected that the County Contacts will be instrumental in communicating information about the farm and its work and in interesting black farmers in ELF's findings. The ELF staff also provides paralegal assistance on land problems and in Alabama it retains a small team of lawyers who have become experts in rural land law through their involvement with ELF. With these and other legal experts, ELF prepared booklets dealing with various legal aspects of real property ownership and the County Contacts distribute these booklets and explain their importance. The first such booklet published was *Adverse Possession*. It provided vital information about land rights and obligations and has proved to be highly popular with the County Contacts and with the people with whom they converse. The Mississippi office of ELF supplements these community outreach and educational efforts with a monthly newsletter which carries information of interest to black landowners and black farmers.

It frequently happens that black landowners, faced with foreclosure, are in need of loans. Such cases are referred to ELF via the County Contact, who is often in a position to make a recommendation because he personally knows the family involved. Also, when a family feels that circumstances absolutely oblige it to sell land it notifies the County Contact so that he may refer the sale to possible purchasers, or to ELF, in hopes that it can find a black buyer.

Although much remains to be done to improve the County Contact System, and although it suffers from the usual problems associated with a corps of volunteer workers, there is no doubt that the system is doing a remarkable job in assisting local people in a very concrete way at a minimum cost. It is the nucleus of what could become a major network of community organizers useful for a variety of programs in other areas. Even in its present volunteer format, CCS merits expansion to other counties in Mississippi and Alabama, as well as to other states which are pleading for assistance with their land problems.

TENNESSEE-TOMBIGBEE WATERWAY PROJECT AREA

The Tennessee-Tombigbee Waterway Project is a one-billion-dollar Federal Public Works Project linking the Tombigbee and Tennessee rivers. The Tennessee-Tombigbee Waterway will provide a new inland water route to connect the Port of Mobile with Nashville, the Midwest, and Chicago. When completed for navigation the waterway is expected to substantially increase the commercial, industrial, and agribusiness activity in the northwest Mississippi and southwest Alabama area.

Construction of the 253-mile water route, which is scheduled to last for ten years, is supervised by the U.S. Army Corps of Engineers with the policy authority vested in the Tennessee-Tombigbee Waterway Development Authority. The authority is a five-state group with membership appointed by the governors of the states of Alabama, Mississippi, Florida, Kentucky, and Tennessee.

The Emergency Land Fund, recognizing the impact that the waterway would have on black landowners in the region, joined with a number of other organizations to form the Minority Peoples' Council for the purpose of educating and organizing the minority population in affected counties. The failure to include any minority representation on the waterway's policy and planning boards despite the fact that 40 percent of the population in the project area is black pointed up the urgency of organizing a bloc for mobilizing community interest.

In addition to its initiative in helping to create the Minority Peoples' Council, ELF undertook an inventory of black landowners in the waterway project area, completing more than 1,200 interviews in four Mississippi counties and involving 85,000 acres of black-owned land. The data collected thus far reveal among other things:

1. A majority of black landowners are not aware of the waterway project.
2. Of those black landowners who are aware of the project, they have learned of it indirectly and in some cases through the inquiries of real estate brokers and speculators that ELF assumed are active (given the anticipated increase in land values associated with the further development of the waterway project).
3. As little as 15 percent of the black landholdings are productively utilized, with some holdings without even a home garden.
4. A majority of the landowners are either not aware of programs offered by FmHA or have not bothered to inquire about such programs.
5. Most of the landowners are fifty-five years or older and their children have moved from the area.

The ELF has operated on the assumption that land not in active use is likely to be lost and that black land in the path of general economic development has a higher probability of being lost than land elsewhere. This is the case with black land in the Tennessee-Tombigbee Waterway Project area. For example, in two Mississippi counties where ELF interviewed black landowners, it was noted that over a five-year period, black landownership had been reduced by 40 percent in Clay County, and 22 percent in Lowndes County; that is, over a five-year period since the 1969 Agricultural Census, black landownership had been reduced from 18,959 acres to 11,376 in Clay County and from 25,588 acres to 18,959 acres in Lowndes County. This alarming rate of decline in black landownership far exceeds recent rates of decline of black-owned land in other areas of the South, and the difference is attributed to the active development of the waterway project.

The survey also served as an educational tool to alert the community to the coming of the waterway and to make residents aware of its implications for their area. The data collected on the characteristics and usage of the black-owned land may later prove valuable for siting development projects of various types.

THE NATIONAL ASSOCIATION OF BLACK LANDOWNERS

From its outset it was apparent that the ELF program had touched a very sensitive chord within the black community, for the response to its appearance was nothing short of remarkable. As word of ELF's existence began to seep out to the community there first emerged a trickle of letters, calls, and personal inquiries. Gradually, that trickle became a veritable torrent, ranging from heartrending pleas for help to very businesslike requests for precise types of assistance to meet very specific situations. Blacks in the North called to inquire whether ELF could save the 50 acres a grandparent had left them, or whether it could suggest what they should do with 120 acres which their relatives had inherited. From the rural South came laboriously handwritten letters describing in agonizing human terms despicable actions which had been perpetrated on the writer as regards his/her land and asking ELF's help. Articles about ELF in the *New York Times* and in *Ebony* served to stimulate this flow, further overtaxing the program's very limited capability to deal with what was clearly emerging as an enormous and highly complex problem long overdue for attention.

Whereas ELF was qualified to do business in seven southern states, it chose to limit itself at the outset to only three: Alabama, Mississippi, and South Carolina. (The national headquarters is in Atlanta but no field office exists in Georgia.) Scarcity of funds, combined with the burgeoning demands for ELF's services, led to a decision to concentrate efforts even further and in 1975, the South Carolina office was closed. It was ELF's hope that some other organizations, perhaps better funded, might take an interest in the black land-loss problem. This did occur in a couple of states on a very limited scale, but the complexities of dealing with the problem apparently discouraged organizations from seriously addressing the land-loss issue and ELF continued to be beseiged by requests from states where it had no staff capability whatsoever.

As a partial means of responding to these expressed needs ELF, together with the Alabama Center for Higher Education, a consortium of the eight senior black colleges in Alabama, sponsored a southwide black landowners' conference. Convened in June 1976 at Tuskegee Institute, the conference was reminiscent of one at Tuskegee in 1891, when black farmers met to discuss problems of blacks in agriculture in general and black landownership in particular.

Five southern states were represented at the conference, which was attended by 150 black landowners who collectively owned in excess of 10,000 acres of land. Conference workshops included discussions of heir property, wills, beef and hog production, crop management, capital needs, forestry and timber management, and oil, gas, and mineral rights. A number of creative ideas emerged, all centering on organized action such as pooling land as collateral for membership loans, collective negotiation of lease arrangements for exploration of oil and mineral possibilities, and group political action on land-related issues. A decision was made to form a National Association of Black Landowners (NABL) which would be a service organization for black landowners—providing educational and legal information, land development and management guidance, assistance in obtaining loans, and generally the full range of services which ELF presently provides in the counties where it is active. The NABL is thus a structure designed to fulfill the ELF function in those areas where ELF is absent. The obvious difficulties of implementing such a plan are apparent, for in effect NABL proposes to become another ELF, but without either its resources or technical skills. The determination of these black landowners to help themselves was made quite explicit, however, when they voted for an annual dues payment of not less than $50 per member! (Many, although certainly not all, of these persons live at the poverty level or below.)

Whether this incipient organization will get off the ground or not remains to be seen. Regional follow-up meetings took place in several areas and a second conference was held in December 1976. Clearly, a need exists and a will has been expressed to address this need. The ELF will continue to do what it can to assist the effort for obviously neither the technical skills nor the volume of resources required is likely to be found within the group itself.

CONCLUSION

The scope and dimensions of declining black landownership are wide and multifaceted. It is a problem which cuts across the domains of economics, of politics, of sociology, and perhaps even of ethics. It is a problem which, if ignored, could lead to a virtually landless black citizenry in a dozen years. (Blacks are currently losing more than 300,000 acres each year.)

Some portion of this land loss is undoubtedly a reflection of the personal preference of individuals to live in cities rather than in rural areas, a phenomenon which is well documented and which is not limited to blacks. The urbanization of America is not a trend which ELF is pretending to reverse.

On the other hand, there is ample evidence that many who are abandoning the land are doing so only because of economic necessity. The ELF addresses itself to those cases, and they are sufficiently numerous to warrant the existence of an organization many times larger than ELF; clearly, ELF is only scratching the surface in the few counties in which it operates. The ELF is not equipped to carry out a cost-benefit anlysis of its program, and much of what it accomplishes does not lend itself to a dollars-and-cents evaluation. How does one place a value on an injustice which has been thwarted or a spirit which has been given hope? One can, however, identify tens of thousands of acres of land which remain in their owners' hands today which, without ELF, would have been in the hands of others, of whites, usually without fair payment having been made.

When agencies such as the FmHA are pressured into extending their services to blacks, when blacks achieve the self-confidence to appear at the tax and partition sales, to bid for their land, and to demand to inspect the county tax records, a positive service is being rendered to the entire community. Citizenship is being made a reality where it had previously been a sham.

As the nation enters an era when food may be a far more vital resource than it has been and when energy-intensive agriculture may become less attractive, the fact that black farmers have been taught to cultivate profitably their small acreages may prove to be a national as well as a personal advantage. This resource advantage is over and above the microeconomic benefit which accrues to the farmer in the form of a higher cash income.

Finally, with the Southeast region, home of more than half of America's black population, enjoying unprecedented prosperity and development—a development which is transforming its economic profile and drastically affecting its land values in numerous ways—it is imperative that the interests of the black landowner not be ridden roughshod. Secretary of Commerce Richardson has released a vital study, *Land and Minority Enterprise: The Crisis and the Opportunity*,[3] which points up, from the business perspective, the importance of land as the major capital asset of the black population. These findings complement and undergird the program of ELF.

Thus, for a mixture of economic and noneconomic and for measurable and nonmeasurable reasons, the program of the Emergency Land Fund is a particularly significant one.

NOTES

1. Robert S. Browne, *Only Six Million Acres: A Decline of Black Owned Land in the Rural South* (New York: The Black Economic Research Center, 1973).

2. Jim Hightower, *Hard Tomatoes, Hard Times: The Failure of the Land-Grant College Complex* (Washington, D.C.: Agribusiness Accountability Project, 1972).

3. U.S., Department of Commerce, *Land and Minority Enterprise: The Crisis and the Opportunity* (Washington, D.C.: Office of Minority Enterprise, 1976).

chapter 9

INSTITUTIONAL PROCEDURES FOR RESOLVING TAX DELINQUENCY IN THE SOUTH

James A. Lewis

INTRODUCTION

Recent studies by Browne and Salamon have documented the steady decline in farmland owned by minorities in the South.[1] Most land titles transferred by minorities are the result of voluntary transactions. However, cases involving other types of transfers have been cited.[2] These include interstate settlements, mortgage foreclosures, partition sales, and tax sales.

This chapter interprets state statutes in the South dealing with tax-delinquent real property, including the institutional setting, process, mechanism, and administration of tax sales. It is not, however, a legal treatise. Although the interpretation of state statutes has been reviewed by many state commissioners, this chapter is not a substitute for legal advice.[3] Legal advice should be sought from an attorney.

There are no statistics available which indicate the frequency of tax sales. Delinquent taxes probably constitute less than 4 percent of a locality's total levy.[4] Some delinquencies are contested assessments which go through an abatement proceding. There are few other cases which eventually result in tax sales.[5]

Despite their infrequency, however, tax sales are of interest because they are a process by which ownership can be transferred. As an initial point of inquiry the following questions might be raised. Do the rules, statutes, or other legal determinants to rights and duties in property vary from one state to another? Are there specific rules which can be identified and analyzed?

Following are some basic assumptions, a description of procedures followed in tax sales, and the classification of tax sale systems into two types. Short summaries of basic procedures in each of the southern states are also given. Finally, implications for future research are included.

BASIC ASSUMPTIONS

As an illustration, let us assume that an owner has not paid his property taxes, that an abatement proceeding is not undertaken, and that taxes are not ever paid by the delinquent owner or his representative. Thus, from the onset of delinquency, a trace can be made of the sequence of events, charges, interests, costs, possession, and time involved throughout the tax sale procedure until ownership of the land is transferred. Assumed also is that land is transferred to private parties and not to the state or local government. Other special provisions exist for the management and disposition of publicly acquired land. In every state the delinquent owner may pay taxes, charges, interest, and costs which have accrued at any date prior to the final transfer of ownership and clear title to the land.

GENERAL PROCEDURES

Technically, taxes are delinquent if they are not paid on their due date. However, most states do not immediately commence tax sale proceedings the day after taxes are due. Generally, there is a period of time ranging from three to ten months in which back taxes plus a penalty or interest charge may be paid. After this period expires, the local government is required to take action.

Most states sell a tax lien or certificate to some private party. This is done to minimize the loss of local revenue. Costs to the government are added to the amount due, the interest, and charges. No doubt, some property owners may use this time period between due date and initiation of the tax sale as a public loan. The amount of charges, interest, penalties, and costs which are assessed in each state will determine if the property owner's decision was economic. Generally, deferring payments and absorbing the additional charges is not a wise decision; however, the decision to defer payment also depends upon the owner's opportunity cost.

When taxes are not paid within the specified time period, the official process for a tax sale begins. The owner generally receives either a personal or a public notice. Some states do not require a personal visit but all have at least one public notice. Through this notice the owner is informed of his delinquency and the amount of taxes, interest, penalties, and costs due; he is informed that failure to pay by a certain date will result in a tax sale. The tax sale is an effort on the part of government to collect its revenue by selling an interest or lien to some other private party. This private party or purchaser of the tax certificate pays the delinquent's debt and then holds a lien on the property. The amount of time from the tax certificate sale until actual title is transferred from the delinquent owner is the redemption period.

Incentives used to attract purchasers include favorable rates of return on investment, possession of property, or first options to ownership of property in the event that the delinquent owner fails to redeem. To return revenues to the locality and maintain property in private ownership, a concerted effort is made to protect the delinquent owner and provide him with an opportunity to retain ownership. In most cases the property owner redeems his property, but in a few title is eventually transferred to another party. The specific procedure depends upon the state in which the property is located. A summary of general procedures used by the southern states appears in table 9.1

TAX SALE SYSTEMS

There are two main categories of tax sale procedures, the "two-sale" system and the "one-sale" system.[6] In the former a tax certificate on back taxes, interest, penalties, and costs is first sold. Then, after a redemption period has expired a second sale is held. At the second sale title to the land is actually sold, normally by auction to the highest bidder. The one-sale system has four basic subclassifications: (1) the bid-down sale, (2) the public auction sale, (3) the tax-sale-no-bid-down, and (4) an automatic sale to the state.

In the bid-down sale the tax certificate goes to the party who agrees to pay taxes, interest, and accrued costs and will accept the lowest rate of interest on investment. Title to the property is granted to the purchaser after the redemption period expires. Under the public auction sale, a tax certificate is granted to the highest bidder; he receives the first option of obtaining title to the property after expiration of the redemption period.

TABLE 9.1 **General Process for Resolving Tax Delinquency in the South***

STATE	Time between due date and delinquency date	Time between delinquency date and date of sale	Charge assessed on amount delinquent (+ costs)	Number of *personal* notices given	Type of tax sale	Amount of delinquent's land sold
Two-sale						
Florida	5 months	1 month estimate	18% annually	none	auction to person bidding lowest rate of interest	all
Kentucky	4 months	6 months estimate	6% of amount due	1	"first-come, first-served"	all
North Carolina	4 months	5 months estimate	2% of amount due plus ¾% monthly	none	auction to highest bidder	all
One-sale						
Alabama	3 months	4 months estimate	6% annually	1	public auction to highest bidder	portion or all

STATE	Time between due date and delinquency date	Time between delinquency date and date of sale	Charge assessed on amount delinquent (+ costs)	Number of *personal* notices given	Type of tax sale	Amount of delinquent's land sold
Mississippi	6 months	6 months estimate	.5% monthly	none	public auction to highest bidder	portion or all
Georgia	3 months	3 months estimate	7% annually	1	public auction to highest bidder	all
South Carolina	3 months	9 months	up to 25% of amount due	1	public auction to highest bidder	all
Tennessee	3 months	8 months estimate	10% of amount due	1	public auction to highest bidder	all

139

T.9.1 continued

STATE	Time between due date and delinquency date	Time between delinquency and date of sale	Charge assessed on amount delinquent (+ costs)	Number of *personal* notices given	Type of tax sale	Amount of delinquent's land sold
Texas	4 months	8 months estimate	8% of amount due + 6% annually	1	public auction to highest bidder	all
Arkansas	8 months	6 weeks estimate	10% of amount due	none	public auction to person paying amount due for the smallest portion of land	portion or all

140

T.9.1 continued

STATE	Time between due date and delinquency date	Time between delinquency and date of sale	Charge assessed on amount delinquent (+ costs)	Number of *personal* notices given	Type of tax sale	Amount of delinquent's land sold
Louisiana	5 months	5 months estimate	10% annually	1	public auction to person paying amount due for the smallest portion of land	portion or all
Oklahoma	3 months	10 months	1% monthly	1	"drawing" if more than one bidder	all
Virginia	9 months	3 years	5% of amount due on first six months. 8% annually thereafter	2	public auction to highest bidder	portion or all

T.9.1.continued

STATE	Receiver of excess proceeds of sale	Interest earned by purchase of tax sale	Possessor of land during redemption period	Length of redemption period	How title is vested if land is not redeemed
Two-sale Florida	no excess	18% or less annually	owner	2 years	second-sale land sold to highest bidder
Kentucky	no excess	12% annually	owner	3 years	second-sale land sold to highest bidder
North Carolina	owner	9% annually	owner	6 months	second-sale land sold to highest bidder
One-sale Alabama	owner	6% annually	purchaser	3 years	automatically to purchaser
Mississippi	owner	5% of amount due + % monthly	owner	2 years	automatically to purchaser

STATE	Receiver of excess proceeds of sale	Interest earned by purchase of tax sale	Possessor of land during redemption period	Length of redemption period	How title is vested if land is not redeemed
Georgia	owner	10% annually	owner	1 year	automatically to purchaser
South Carolina	owner	8% or 12% annually depending on when redeemed	owner	1.5 years	automatically to purchaser
Tennessee	state	6% annually	purchaser	2 years	automatically to purchaser
Texas	owner	25% or 50% of amount due depending upon when redeemed	owner	2 years	automatically to purchaser
Arkansas	no excess	10% annually	owner	2 years	automatically to purchaser

T.9.1 continued

STATE	Receiver of excess proceeds of sale	Interest earned by purchase of tax sale	Possessor of land during redemption period	Length of redemption period	How title is vested if land is not redeemed
Louisiana	no excess	5% of purchase price plus 1% monthly	purchaser	3 years	automatically to purchaser
Oklahoma	no excess	8% annually	owner	2 years	automatically to purchaser
Virginia	owner	none	lessee	3 years	automatically to highest bidder at the sale

Tax delinquency may be resolved at any time prior to expiration of the redemption period by paying all accrued taxes, interest, charges, and costs. This table has been developed to follow the process through to the transfer of title from the delinquent taxpayer to another private party. If there are no private parties who will invest their funds, the land goes to the state. Provisions for management and disposal of properties reverted to the state have been omitted from this analysis. States are presented in order of similar types of tax sale systems.

144

Tax-sale-no-bid-down is one in which the purchaser bids on the smallest tract for which he will pay the total taxes, interest, and costs. First option for title to the land goes to the purchaser after the redemption period has expired. Automatic sales to the state is a system in which the state assumes control over the property and usually passes ownership back to private parties in accordance with state statutes.

Florida, Kentucky, and North Carolina have two-sale systems for resolving property tax delinquency. Alabama, Arkansas, Georgia, Louisiana, Mississippi, Oklahoma, South Carolina, Tennessee, Texas, and Virginia have one-sale systems.

TWO-SALE STATES

Generally, two-sale states first sell a tax certificate to a private party. This amounts to an interest-bearing investment for the purchaser of the tax certificate. His investment is the amount of taxes, charges, and costs which are due the local government. At the end of the redemption period a second sale is held. At the second sale title to the land is auctioned off to the highest bidder—who may or may not be the tax certificate purchaser. The lowest acceptable bid is the amount of the tax certificate plus interest and costs.

FLORIDA

Approximately five months after taxes are due in November the procedure for tax sale is under way in Florida. A charge of 18 percent annual interest is automatically assessed on April 1. Four public notices are given prior to the tax sale which is before the first of June. Public notice includes place, date of sale, description of the property, and the amount of taxes, interest, and costs due. At the tax sale purchasers pay only the amount of taxes, interest, and costs accrued. Bidding is entered on the lowest rate of interest which the purchaser will accept with an upper limit of 18 percent annually. Actually, bidders begin at 18 percent and bid down. The prospective purchaser who bids the lowest rate of interest is awarded the tax certificate. Thus the Florida system is the reverse of the traditional auction.

After a redemption period of approximately two years a second sale is held. The delinquent owner retains posession of the property during the

redemption period. At the second sale, title to the property is transferred
to the highest cash bidder. The minimum acceptable bid is the amount
due on the tax certificate, costs, and 1.5 percent interest for one month.
If no one bids the purchaser of the tax certificate is assumed to be the
highest bidder and is awarded title to the property.

KENTUCKY

In Kentucky taxes are due on September 15 and if they are not paid by
January 1, a 2 percent charge is added to the amount due. If they remain
unpaid by February 1, the charge becomes 6 percent of the total amount.
At least one personal notice by mail is sent to the delinquent owner in
addition to three public notices. Interest on the tax sale certificate is
fixed at 12 percent annually and only the amount of taxes, interest, and
costs due are accepted in the bidding. The first purchaser to offer to pay
cash is awarded the certificate. If there is more than one offer, the
purchaser with the most recent claim against the delinquent or the property is awarded the certificate.

The delinquent owner retains possession of the property throughout
the two-year redemption period. At the second sale title to the property
is auctioned to the highest bidder with a minimum acceptable bid
amounting to accrued taxes, interest, and costs. If there are no competing bidders at the second sale, then title is automatically vested in the
tax certificate purchaser.

NORTH CAROLINA

In North Carolina taxes are due September 1 and are considered
delinquent if they are not paid by the following January 1. If paid during
January, a 2 percent interest charge is assessed. After January 31, .75
percent monthly interest is added to the amount due. Four public notices
are given prior to the tax certificate sale. The last notice includes date,
time, place, purpose of sale, name of the landowner, description of the
land, and the amount due.

The certificate is granted to the highest bidder at the sale with a
minimum acceptable bid of taxes, interest, and accrued costs. All of the
parcel upon which taxes are delinquent is included in the tax certificate.
Interest on investment for the purchaser is set at 9 percent annually.

After a six-month redemption period the second sale is held, at which time title to the property is auctioned to the highest bidder. The minimum acceptable bid is taxes, interest, and costs which have accrued. If no one bids at this second sale, title is transferred to the purchaser of the tax certificate.

ONE-SALE STATES

Most of the one-sale states have a public auction to the highest bidder. There are, however, different variations of this system which make each state somewhat unique. The delinquent taxpayer is usually informed prior to the final date of expiration of the redemption period.

ALABAMA AND MISSISSIPPI

Alabama and Mississippi hold a public auction to the highest bidder. The smallest portion of land which will bring the amount of taxes, interest, and costs due is auctioned. The other one-sale states hold a public auction to the highest bidder and automatically sell a lien on all of the delinquent parcel.

Taxes are due on October 1 and are delinquent if not paid by January 1 in Alabama. A 6 percent interest charge is assessed on delinquent taxes. The delinquent owner receives one personal notice by visit or mail before the tax sale is held. At the sale potential purchasers are attracted by a 6-percent interest on investment and possession of the property during the three-year redemption period. The delinquent owner pays for any improvements made on the property during the redemption period. If property is not redeemed, then the purchaser at the tax sale is automatically awarded title to the property.

In Mississippi taxes are due in three installments. Half is due on February 1, one quarter on May 1, and the final quarter is due on August 1. Failure to make any of the installments initiates the tax sale process. Charges on the delinquent balance are assessed at 5 percent per month. Delinquent owners receive a public notice which includes date, time, place, name of the owner, description of the property, and the amount due. At the sale as much of the land is auctioned to the highest bidder as is needed to assure that the taxes, interest, and costs accrued are raised. Forty acres or a smaller subdivision is first offered. Purchasers receive 5 percent interest plus 1 percent per month over the two-year redemption period. The delinquent owner retains possession of the property and does not pay for any improvements made to the property by the purchaser.

GEORGIA, SOUTH CAROLINA, TENNESSEE, AND TEXAS

What is common to Georgia, South Carolina, Tennessee, and Texas is that a public auction is held and the entire parcel is included in the tax certificate.

In Georgia, taxes are due January 1 and are delinquent if not paid by April 1. After April 1, a charge of 7 percent is added to the bill. The owner receives one personal notice by mail or visit prior to the sale. Purchasers are attracted to the sale by a 10 percent interest on investment. Any excess over the amount of taxes, interest, and costs are remitted to the delinquent owner. After a twelve-month redemption period the purchaser can obtain title to the property.

Tax assessments are sent to owners in October and are due on January 1 in South Carolina. If the taxes are not paid by January 15 a 15 percent charge is assessed; after March 15 an additional 5 percent is assessed, and after September 1 another 5 percent is added. Tax sales are held in October and delinquent property is auctioned to the highest bidder. There is an eighteen-month redemption period during which the delinquent owner retains possession of the property. The purchaser receives 8 percent interest on investment if the land is redeemed in twelve months. If redemption is made in the last six months, then the interest is 12 percent annually. Failure to redeem results in title to the land being transferred to the tax sale purchaser.

In Tennessee, taxes are due in October and are delinquent if not paid by the following January. Counties with populations of 600,000 or more assess a charge of .5 percent per month on the amount due after January 15. Counties with less than 600,000 population assess the .5 percent charge after March 1. When the county files suit for tax sale, usually after April 1, a 10 percent charge is attached to the amount due. Delinquent owners are sent a personal notice by mail informing them of the impending sale. At the tax sale, a public auction to the highest bidder is held. The purchaser receives possession of the property over the two-year redemption period and 6 percent return on investment. The delinquent owner pays for any improvements made on the property during the redemption period. If the taxes, interest, and costs due on the land are not paid by the end of the redemption period, then the purchaser at the tax sale becomes the owner.

Texas allows the owner to pay taxes between October 1 and January 31, after which time they are considered delinquent. However, if half of the taxes are paid by November 3, then the remaining balance is not delinquent until the next July 1. Delinquent taxes bear an interest charge of 6 percent annually from the date of delinquency. An additional penalty is assessed depending upon when payment is made. If taxes are paid in February, the rate is 1 percent; if in March, 2 percent; if in April, 3 percent; if in May, 4 percent; if in June, 5 percent; and if after July, an 8 percent charge is assessed. The delinquent owner is provided one personal notice of the tax sale by mail. Around the first of September a public auction is held selling the tax certificate to the highest bidder. Any excess over the amount of taxes, interest, and costs due goes to the delinquent owner, who also retains possession of the property over the two-year redemption period. If redemption is made in the first year, the purchaser receives 25 percent interest on investment and if during the second year, a 50 percent rate is received. Failure to redeem results in the purchaser obtaining title to the property.

ARKANSAS AND LOUISIANA

In Arkansas taxes are due between the third Monday in February and October 10, after which time they are delinquent and assessed a 10 percent additional charge. Tax sales are held in late November and delinquent owners are given public notice. At the sale only bids for the taxes, interest, and costs due are accepted. Purchasers bid on the smallest tract of land for which they will pay the amount due with a set 10 percent annual rate of return on investment. After a two-year redemption period, in which the delinquent owner retains possession of the property, title is passed to the tax sale purchaser.

Louisiana has a system very similar to that of neighboring Arkansas. A 10 percent charge is assessed on unpaid taxes after December 31. Delinquent owners receive one personal notice by mail or visit prior to the tax sale which is sometime before May 1. Purchasers at the tax sale pay only the amount due. Interest earned on investment is a flat 5 percent plus 1 percent per month over the three-year redemption period. The purchaser also obtains possession of the property and is compensated for any improvements which are made if the delinquent owner redeems his property. If redemption is not made, then the purchaser obtains title.

OKLAHOMA AND VIRGINIA

The due date for taxes in Oklahoma is November 1 and if they are not paid by January 1, they become delinquent. An interest charge of 1 percent per month is assessed on delinquent taxes. If half of the taxes are paid prior to January 1, the balance does not become delinquent until April 1. If taxes are still delinquent the following September, then the tax sale procedure begins. The delinquent owner receives one personal notice by mail. Tax sales are held the first Monday in October with taxes, interest, and costs due being the only acceptable bid. If more than one prospective purchaser bids, then a fair and impartial drawing is held. An 8 percent annual interest on investment is awarded the purchaser. The delinquent owner retains possession of the property over the two-year redemption period. At the expiration of the redemption period the purchaser is awarded title to the property.

Real property taxes are due on December 5 in Virginia, after which time they are considered delinquent and are assessed a 5 percent interest charge. If taxes are not paid by the following June 30, an additional 8 percent is charged. In Virginia only one sale is held but it does not occur until after three years from the time taxes are delinquent. When the sale does occur title to the land is auctioned to the highest bidder. Only the smallest portion of a parcel which will bring the taxes, interest, and costs due is sold. During the three-year redemption period, the local treasurer may lease the delinquent property to another private party. The duration of the lease is one year and the rent must equal taxes, interest, and costs. Such leases are renewable and may be arranged either with private parties or issued at public auction, whichever is more expedient for the local government.

IMPLICATIONS FOR RESEARCH

Taxation of real property is principally a function of local government. Property taxation constitutes its major source of revenue. Failure to pay property taxes is of serious concern to both owner and local government. Somehow, either through abatement proceedings, payment, or through a tax sale, the delinquency must be resolved. If it is not resolved, then those who do pay taxes are likely to be paying higher taxes if revenues are to be maintained.

Although property taxes are assessed, collected, and spent mostly at the local level, the rules, regulations, and procedures covering the treatment of tax delinquency have been established at the state level. Every state in the South has its own set of rules and regulations, in the form of state statutes, which set forth the process by which tax assessments are to be made and collected. Private owners are obligated to pay property taxes. If these taxes are not paid, the law prescribes a process which government officials must follow to collect the funds. Eventually, this process can culminate in the transfer of title to ownership through a tax sale.

Failing to pay property taxes does not necessarily mean that the owner will unequivocally lose his land. Every state makes a conscientious effort to preserve and protect the rights of delinquent owners. Due process of law is essential. Numerous warnings and opportunities for redemption are given. However, to insure that property is maintained as a local revenue source it is sometimes necessary to transfer ownership.

The systems which exist in each of the states start to function at the time when delinquency occurs. Given a tax-delinquent property, a process exists to deal with the problem from the standpoint of the local government. Its objective is to maintain the revenue-producing capabilities of property for the local government and to maintain that property in private ownership.[7]

The processes which exist are designed to protect the rights of the delinquent owner, to provide a mechanism to collect needed revenues, and to attract investors to provide needed cash for the local government's treasury.

Each state has a different institutional structure. The fact that different institutions exist is not particularly disturbing. It only means that one must be more astute and attentive about different processes, incentives, causes, and economic effects. To attract purchasers some states offer attractive rates of return on investment, others offer possession of property, and others offer the opportunity of short-term ownership acquisition. The speed, ease, and rate of return for purchasers of delinquent land weigh against the protective features of redemption by delinquent taxpayers in determining the "market" for delinquent property.

The system for resolving property tax delinquency in each of the states constitutes different ways of dealing with a similar problem. The rules, regulations, and procedures which have been outlined also define a pricing system. This system is representative of administered pricing, wherein demand and supply adjust to clear the market. Although it may not be very sophisticated or popular to refer to a supply schedule of delinquent properties, there are some factors in addition to low income which could explain the frequency of delinquency. Presumably the primary factor is insufficient income, although some owners may be simply deferring the cash outlay and absorbing the penalties. Low income can be temporary in some cases and chronic in others. Temporary income loss could result from natural diasters which cause crop failures, destruction of capital facilities, livestock losses, and unemployment. Chronic low income could be due to several socioeconomic factors. In addition to race these factors include age, education, occupation, and location. Underemployment, unemployment, low wages, poor quality farmland, inefficient use of land, input cost increases, and interregional competition are additional factors which may be important.[8]

There is obviously a great need for American taxpayers to know more about how the tax institutions function. Therefore, the following questions are presented as possible subject areas for future research:

1. Are there specific socioeconomic characteristics of delinquent owners which can be identified? Characteristics such as age, education, occupation, income, and race would be major factors.

2. Are there specific characteristics of owners who lose their land?

3. Once the process for tax sales has been initiated, is the delinquent caught in a spiralling sequence of events where loss of land is unavoidable?

4. If a change in ownership occurs is there a change in land use? What kind of change in use with what result? In states where a portion of the land is separated to satisfy the tax obligation is the land reduced to an uneconomic-sized unit?

5. What are the effects of the institution on altering wealth and income distribution? Is there a transfer from poor to wealthy? Is the change desirable from the standpoint of society if measured in terms of land use, productivity, income, employment, output, resource allocation, and improved standards of living?

6. Do more complex, roundabout systems (for example, those with many built-in "protective mechanisms") tend to favor those with greater legal and economic resources?
7. Who are the investors (purchasers) of tax-delinquent properties? Are they predominately speculators, developers, or occasional investors who periodically subsidize their neighbors in times of economic stress?
8. What are the principal incentives for purchases? High rates of return, possession, short-term acquisition, low-risk investment and low-cost acquisitions are incentives used in different combinations. How sensitive (response elasticity) are investors to changes of differences in incentive systems?
9. Are there community factors which might indicate a high probability of tax delinquency? If so, what kind of policy actions might be taken to lower the probability of delinquency?
10. What portion of tax-delinquent properties end up in tax sales?
11. Is tax delinquency a repetitive phenomenon for either the parcel or the owner?
12. Are the different stage systems effective in resolving local needs for revenue?
13. Is there a preferred cost-effective system?
14. Do administrative and legal costs vary from state to state?
15. And, finally, are the information systems meeting the needs of assessor, recorder, commissioner of revenue, and property owner?

These questions illustrate needs and possibilities for future research. Such research should focus on the three major participants in this process—government, delinquent owner, and investor—and three economic fundamentals of the system—price determination, productivity, and allocation. The results of research along these lines should surface better and more comprehensive answers.

NOTES

1. Robert S. Browne, *Only Six Million Acres: A Decline of Black Owned Land in the Rural South* (New York: The Black Economic Research Center, 1973); and Lester M. Salamon, *Black-Owned Land: Profile of a Disappearing Equity Base* (Washington, D.C.: Office of Minority Business Enterprise, U.S. Department of Commerce, 1974).

2. Ibid.

3. Reviews have been received from Virginia, Kentucky, North Carolina, Florida, Mississippi, Louisiana, Arkansas, and Oklahoma.

4. Two studies show that the average delinquency is just under 4 percent of the total billings: *Property Tax Delinquency in Minnesota,* Minnesota Department of Revenue, Research Report no. 123, March 1976, and a special study on "Local Property Tax Delinquency" conducted by Division of Research, Virginia State Department of Taxation, Richmond, Va., November 1971.

5. In the U.S. in 1976, the average number of transfers was 42.7 per 1,000 farms. Thirty-four point four per 1,000 farms were voluntary and estate settlements, 1.5 per 1,000 farms were loss of title by default of contract, sale to avoid mortgage foreclosure, surrender of title, or other transfers to avoid mortgage foreclosure. The remaining 6.8 transfers per 1,000 farms were mostly the result of inheritance and gifts; however, this category also includes tax sales and other miscellaneous and unclassified sales. *Farm Real Estate Market Developments,* U.S. Department of Agriculture, CD-81, July 1976, table 14, p. 23.

6. Howard C. Emmerman, "Legislating Protection of the Delinquent Property Owner in an Era of Super-Marketable Tax Titles," *DePaul Law Review* 19, no. 2 (Winter 1969).

7. George V. Voinovich, "The CURE Proposal: Planning for Industrial Redevelopment," *International Assessor* 42, no. 8 (August 1976), p. 3. Voinovich also indicates that the administrative cost for processing a tax sale in the Cleveland, Ohio, area is $500 per parcel. Only 5 percent of all parcels sold recoup the full cost. Also, 60 percent of the parcels sold in tax sales in 1969 and 1972 were delinquent again in 1974.

A recent newspaper account for the northern Virginia-metropolitan Washington, D.C., area indicated that about a third of tax-delinquent parcels were left over after development or could not be located. Since this amounts to over $2.37 million in Fairfax County, about $277,000 in Arlington County, and $877,000 in Alexandria, one might question the functioning of information systems. Although a portion of these dollars is delinquent personal property and the total rate of delinquency is 2.8 percent of the total levy, the revenue loss is no small matter. If these revenues could be captured, cost effectively, there might be a noticeable difference in public services—education, for example.

8. Community growth is another event which can bring additional tax liability for landowners. An increase in population implies greater demands for space and public services. These demands will eventually be reflected in total levies. Some owners may not be able to keep pace with the rate of growth in their total tax bill and experience increased difficulty in meeting their needs.

chapter 10

THE FUTURE OF BLACK LAND IN THE SOUTH*

Lester M. Salamon

INTRODUCTION

One of the most persistent barriers to minority economic development
in the United States has been the lack of capital under minority control.
The president's Advisory Council on Minority Business Enterprise took
explicit note of this fact in 1971 when it reported to the president that:
"Economic development cannot proceed without a financial base."[1] To
remedy this situation, the advisory council proposed a new strategy for
minority business development activities, one that focused on "expanded ownership" of equity resources.

Fortunately, this new emphasis has finally attracted attention to a
minority equity resource and a group of minority entrepreneurs that
have long been ignored in federal minority development efforts:
minority-owned land and the farmers and other businessmen who control it. In the South at least, blacks and other minorities own millions of
acres of land, making land probably the largest single equity resource in
minority hands in the region.

This chapter will identify some of the major characteristics of black
land inheritance, analyze the socioeconomic and political impact of
landownership, and explore some ideas for a land-based minority enterprise strategy. Part 1 examines the basic contours of black-owned land
in the South—its scope, location, structure, recent trends, and profitability. Part 2 summarizes the results of an evaluation of the long-term

*Adapted from Lester M. Salamon, *Land and Minority Enterprise: The Crisis and
The Opportunity* (Washington, D.C.: U.S. Government Printing Office, 1976).
The author wishes to express his appreciation to the Office of Minority Business
Enterprise of the U.S. Department of Commerce for financial support that made
the research reported here possible.

impact of the New Deal's resettlement program which made parcels of land available for purchase by several thousand black sharecroppers in the South during the late 1930s. Out of this study comes some documentation of the actual effect that landownership has in producing social and economic—not to mention political—change. Finally, Part 3 explores one relatively inexpensive component of a possible land-based minority enterprise development policy, a component that would involve greater utilization by minority landowners of publicly owned lands in their regions, especially those publicly owned lands already put to commercial use.

THE SCOPE AND CHARACTER OF MINORITY LAND RESOURCES

At the time of the 1969 Census of Agriculture, black farm landowners—including both full owners and part owners—numbered 66,815 out of a total farm landowner population of 1,059,914 in the fourteen states of the South. As noted in table 10.1, these black landowners farmed over 5.5 million acres of land, out of 282 million acres farmed by all landowners in the region.

Much of this black-controlled land is concentrated in a handful of states. As of 1969, for example, Mississippi alone accounted for almost one-quarter of the black farm landowners in the region. Four states— Alabama, Mississippi, North Carolina, and South Carolina—account for almost 60 percent of all black farm landowners and 52 percent of all black-controlled land (see table 10.2).

Although blacks constitute only slightly more than 6 percent of all farm landowners in the South, they comprise a much more substantial proportion of all landowners in these several states. In Mississippi and South Carolina, for example, more than 20 percent of all farm landowners are black. In Alabama, Louisiana, and North Carolina, about 10 percent are black. In none of these states, however, is the acreage held by blacks proportional to the number of black landowners. This pattern points to one of the central characteristics of black-owned farms in the South: their relatively small size. Only in Missouri, where there are few black-owned farms, does the average size of the farms of black full owners reach even 60 percent of the average size of the farms of *all* full owners. Elsewhere, black full-owned and part-owned farms are typi-

TABLE 10.1 **Extent of Black Landownership in 14 Southern States, 1969**

	Total		Black Full Owners		Black Part Owners	
	Nonwhite Landowners	As % of All Landowners	Total Number	As % of All Full Owners	Total Number	As % of All Part Owners
Number	66,815	6.3%	51,757	6.32%	15,058	6.23%
Acres	5,640,962	2.0	3,779,317	2.56	1,859,645	1.38
Acres per farm	84.5	31.7	73.0	40.6	124.2	22.2

TABLE 10.2 **Distribution of Black Farm Landowners and Acres of Black-Owned Farmland among 14 Southern States, 1969**

	Total Black Landowners		Black Full Owners				Black Part Owners			
	Number	%	Number	%	Acres	%	Number	%	Acres	%
Alabama	7,226	10.8	5,486	10.6	440,791	11.7	1,740	11.6	196,078	10.5
Arkansas	3,013	4.5	2,153	4.2	139,029	3.7	860	5.7	147,186	7.9
Florida	1,243	1.9	953	1.8	78,043	2.1	290	1.9	55,334	3.0
Georgia	4,450	6.7	3,477	6.7	403,463	10.7	973	6.5	175,010	9.4
Kentucky	1,585	2.4	1,341	2.6	82,105	2.2	244	1.6	24,176	1.3
Louisiana	3,884	5.8	3,034	5.9	170,838	4.5	850	5.6	102,942	5.5
Mississippi	14,527	21.7	12,222	23.6	949,310	25.1	2,305	15.3	313,042	16.7
Missouri	358	0.5	282	0.5	32,987	0.9	76	0.5	14,212	0.8
North Carolina	9,687	14.5	7,107	13.7	373,929	9.8	2,580	17.2	184,932	9.8
South Carolina	7,514	11.2	5,595	10.8	310,371	8.2	1,919	12.7	169,674	9.1
Tennessee	3,890	5.8	2,998	5.8	182,624	4.8	892	5.9	102,611	5.5
Texas	4,747	7.1	3,720	7.2	357,538	9.5	1,027	6.8	222,120	11.9
Virginia	4,646	7.0	3,356	6.5	255,054	6.7	1,290	8.6	155,620	8.3
West Virginia	45	0.1	33	0.1	3,233	0.1	12	0.1	6,708	0.3
Total	66,815	100.0	51,757	100.0	3,779,315	100.0	15,058	100.0	1,869,645	100.0

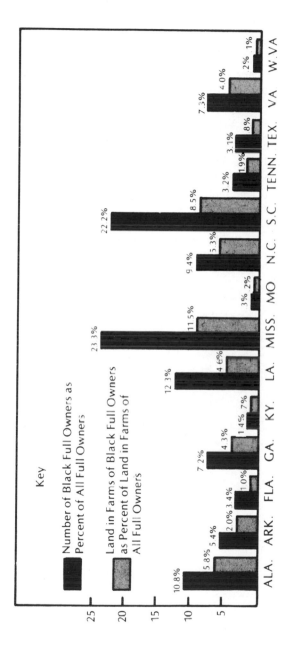

Key

■ Number of Black Full Owners as Percent of All Full Owners

▨ Land in Farms of Black Full Owners as Percent of Land in Farms of All Full Owners

ALA. — 10.8%, 5.8% 5.4%
ARK. — 2.0% 3.4%
FLA. — 7.2%, 1.0%
GA. — 4.3%, 1.4% 7%
KY. — 12.3%, 4.6%
LA. — 23.3%, 11.5%
MISS. — 3% 2%
MO. — 9.4%, 5.3%
N.C. — 22.2%, 8.5%
S.C. — 3.2%, 1.9%
TENN. — 3.1%, 8%
TEX. — 7.3%, 4.0%
VA. — 2% 1%
W.VA.

Black Full Owners as Percent of All Full Owners and as Percent of All Land Owned by All Full Owners in 14 Southern States, 1969

cally only about half as large as all full or part-owned farms. As a result, in every state black landowners account for a significantly smaller share of the *land* owned by all landowners than they do of the *number* of landowners, as figure 3 vividly reveals.

TRENDS IN BLACK LANDOWNERSHIP

Although black land resources are sizable, they have been disappearing at a rapid rate. Between 1954 and 1969, the number of black full owners dropped from about 126,000 to about 52,000—a decline of 59 percent—while the number of black part owners declined from about 50,000 to about 15,000—a decline of about 70 percent (see table 10.3).

TABLE   10.3   **Decline in the Number of Black Landowners and in the Acres in Farms of Black Landowners in 14 Southern States, 1954, 1969**

	Number of Black Landowners			Acres in Farms of Black Landowners		
	1954	*1969*	*% Change*	*1954*	*1969*	*% Change*
Alabama	18,408	7,226	−60.7	1,262,583	636,859	−49.6
Arkansas	9,894	3,013	−69.5	659,081	286,215	−56.6
Florida	4,536	1,243	−72.6	242,530	133,377	−45.0
Georgia	12,049	4,450	−63.1	1,126,378	578,473	−48.6
Kentucky	2,432	1,585	−34.8	129,538	106,281	−18.0
Louisiana	12,783	3,884	−69.6	578,661	273,780	−57.9
Mississippi	27,746	14,527	−47.6	1,971,540	1,262,352	−36.0
Missouri	934	358	−61.7	69,912	47,199	−32.5
North Carolina	22,625	9,687	−57.2	1,085,750	558,861	−48.5
South Carolina	21,670	7,514	−65.3	999,050	480,045	−51.9
Tennessee	7,215	3,890	−46.1	419,591	285,235	−32.0
Texas	18,877	4,747	−74.9	1,184,183	579,658	−51.0
Virginia	15,957	4,646	−70.9	877,100	410,674	−53.2
West Virginia	260	45	−82.7	13,470	9,941	−26.2
Total	175,386	66,815	−61.9	10,619,367	5,648,960	−46.8

Nor do these trends show any sign of abating. During the most recent five-year period for which data is available—1964 to 1969—the number of black full owners declined 24.1 percent, and the number of black part owners plummeted 50.3 percent. Paradoxically, this was the very period when an entire series of active new governmental efforts to assist the poor were inaugurated. Whatever their general effects, these measures seem to have provided little relief to the critically important pool of southern black farmowners whose accumulated savings in the form of land have long constituted the only sizable equity resource available to blacks in the South.

To be sure, white landowners also declined during this fifteen-year period. Yet, black losses were disproportionately large: 15 percent of all full owners who left farming during this period and 32 percent of all part owners who left were blacks, even though blacks comprised only 9.6 percent of all full owners and 14 percent of all part owners in 1954. Whatever the causes of the decline in the number of farm landowners in the South during this period, the effects of these factors were proportionately greater on blacks than on whites.

Not all black farmowners shared equally in this decline, however. The drop was most severe among the smallest black landowners. As a result, there has been a steady rise in the average size of black-owned farms. Between 1954 and 1969, for example, the average acreage of farms of black full owners increased 30 percent, while that of black part owners increased 73 percent. Nevertheless, the typical black-owned farm still constitutes an extremely small-scale operation. As of 1969, for example, the average fully owned black farm, though 30 percent larger than its counterpart fifteen years earlier, was still only 40 percent as large as the average size of all full-owner farms. Black part owners were slightly better off with farms averaging 124 acres (compared to 73 acres for black full owners), but the farms of all part owners were almost five times as large.

Not only has the recent decline of black farmowners hit the smallest owners most severely, but it has also affected the subsistence farmers more extensively than the "commercial" ones.[2] As a result, between 1959 and 1969, while the total number of black-owned farms declined, the proportion of that total represented by commercial farms increased slightly, from 42 percent to 48 percent. This slightly greater durability of black commercial farms was even more striking in the case of the larger commercial farms, those with sales in excess of $2,500. While all black-owned farms declined by 46 percent between 1959 and 1969,

TABLE 10.4   **Changes in the Proportion of Black Part Owners to All Black Landowners, 1954–1969**

	1954	1959	1964	1969	% change 1954–1969	% change 1964–1969
Black Full Owners	125,831	87,118	68,425	51,757	−58.9	−24.3
Black Part Owners	49,555	36,564	30,352	15,051	−69.6	−50.4
All Black Landowners	197,386	123,682	98,777	69,815	−61.9	−32.4
Part Owners as % of total	28.3	29.6	30.7	22.5	−20.5	−26.7

these more substantial commercial farms declined by a considerably smaller 21 percent. As a result, these operations accounted for almost 26 percent of all black-owned farms by 1969, compared to 18 percent ten years earlier.

A third group of black farmowners that has been hit disproportionately hard during the recent drop in black landownership has been the part owners, those operators who own a portion of the land in their farms but lease additional land as well. Farms operated by part owners tend to be larger operations, since the owners have apparently reached out to lease additional land in order to increase the viability of their operations. However, as table 10.4 shows, the number of black part-owners declined 70 percent between 1954 and 1969, while the number of full owners was declining a smaller 57 percent. Curiously, moreover, most of this heavy part-owner loss occurred during the most recent five-year period—1964–1969. This development is especially significant because the opportunity to rent additional land has been a crucial source of staying power for small black landowners. Evidently, this opportunity disappeared at a rapid pace between 1964 and 1969, for reasons that are only partially clear.

A final trend worth noting about black farmowners has to do with their age. As table 10.5 indicates, more than half of all black full owners were over fifty-five years old as of 1964, and this figure rose even further by 1969. Quite clearly, blacks in the most productive age brackets—thirty-five to fifty-four—are leaving the land even more rapidly than black farmers as a whole.

TABLE 10.5 **Change in the Age Structure of Black Full Owners in the South, 1964, 1969**

Age	1964[a]		1969[b]	
	Number	*%*	*Number*	*%*
Under 35	999	3.5	515	5.3
35–54	11,585	40.2	3,489	35.6
55 and over	16,237	56.3	5,788	59.1
Total	28,821	100.0	9,792	100.0

[a]Figures for 1964 are for owners of Class 1-6 farms
[b]Figures for 1969 are for owners of Class 1-5 farms only

ECONOMIC CHARACTERISTICS OF BLACK-OWNED FARM ENTERPRISES: PROFITABILITY AND EFFICIENCY

In view of these trends, how viable is the black land base as a source of capital leveraging power for economic development activities? The ultimate answer to this question, of course, depends on the nature of the changes taking place in the vicinity of black-owned land, as well as on the secureness of the title of black landowners. However, some important clues can be had by looking at the dynamics of black agricultural enterprises.

Fortunately, the Census of Agriculture provides some useful data on this question, although only for the 17,000 out of the total 67,000 black farms that qualify as commercial enterprises. What emerges most clearly from this data is a fascinating and important paradox about black farm enterprises. On the one hand, as table 10.6 shows, black commercial farmers are earning far lower profits *per acre* than all commercial farmers. However, as noted in table 10.7, when these profits are computed on a *per-acre* basis, black commercial farmers turn out to be doing at least as well, and frequently better, than all commercial farmers. For example, in Mississippi in 1969, black full owners earned profits per farm that were only 54 percent as much as those of all full owners. However, profits per acre on black commercial farms were 97 percent as high as profits per acre on the farms of all full owners. The respective figures for North Carolina were 66 percent on a per-farm basis and 111 percent on a per-acre basis. Moreover, the same pattern holds for machinery investment. Alabama black full owners had only 85 percent as much machinery per farm as did all Alabama full owners, but they had 110 percent as much machinery *per acre* as did all Alabama commercial farmers. In short, there is substantial evidence of both the efficiency of small black commercial farms, and of the capital leveraging power of the land in their enterprises. What this seems to suggest is a far greater opportunity than is commonly assumed for viable economic enterprises built on the foundation of minority-owned land.

Thus three conclusions seem to emerge regarding the general pattern of minority landholdings in the South. First, these landholdings are quite substantial, amounting to close to 6 million acres as of 1969. Even conservatively estimated, this results in an equity base of something on

TABLE 10.6   **Income and Expenses per Farm of Black Full Owners and All Full Owners by State, Class 1-5 Farms, 1969**

	Black Full Owners				All Full Owners				Black Average
	1	*2*	*3*	*4*	*5*	*6*	*7*	*8*	Gross Profit as % of All (4÷8)
	Value of Products Sold	Income from Gov't. Programs	Production Expenses	Gross Profit Per Farm [(1+2)−3]	Value of Products Sold	Income from Gov't. Programs	Production Expenses	Gross Profit Per Farm [(5+6)−7]	
Alabama	$9,043	$1,072	$6,889	$3,226	$21,530	$1,317	$18,462	$4,385	73.5
Arkansas	7,401	1,318	6,108	2,611	25,668	1,718	21,948	5,438	48.0
Florida	8,909	937	6,673	3,173	42,426	1,359	36,961	6,824	46.5
Georgia	9,797	971	8,182	2,586	25,501	1,611	21,962	5,150	50.2
Kentucky	7,833	780	5,158	3,455	9,911	866	6,772	4,005	86.3
Louisiana	8,173	930	6,508	2,595	19,760	2,725	16,647	5,838	44.4
Mississippi	8,427	1,274	6,812	2,889	19,452	2,904	17,011	5,345	54.1
Missouri	N.A.	N.A.	N.A.	N.A.	N.A.	N.A.	N.A.	N.A.	N.A.
North Carolina	7,680	464	5,109	3,035	15,962	812	12,145	4,629	65.6
South Carolina	7,635	790	5,248	3,177	15,827	1,584	13,186	4,225	75.2
Tennessee	5,407	961	4,235	2,133	9,726	1,022	7,546	3,202	66.6
Texas	8,302	1,211	6,935	2,578	23,718	2,970	21,899	4,789	53.2
Virginia	6,711	282	3,818	3,175	13,248	533	10,531	3,250	97.7
West Virginia	5,667	—	3,333	2,334	11,927	351	9,540	2,738	85.1

TABLE 10.7   **Income and Expenses per Acre of Black Full Owners and All Full Owners by State, Class 1–5 Farms, 1969**

| | Black Full Owners | | | | All Full Owners | | | | |
| | *1* | *2* | *3* | *4* | *5* | *6* | *7* | *8* | Gross Profit— Black Full Owners as % of All Full Owners |
	Value of Products Sold per Acre	Income from Gov't. Programs per Acre	Production Expenses per Acre	Gross Profit per Acre [(1+2)−3]	Value of Products Sold per Acre	Income from Gov't Programs per Acre	Production Expenses per Acre	Gross Profit per Acre [(5+6)−7]	(4÷8)
Alabama	$43.40	$ 5.14	$33.06	$15.48	$ 80.10	$4.90	$68.71	$16.29	95.0
Arkansas	59.50	10.59	49.10	20.99	96.00	6.42	82.05	20.37	103.0
Florida	52.30	5.50	39.14	18.66	93.60	3.00	81.54	15.06	123.9
Georgia	47.10	4.60	39.36	12.41	86.90	5.49	74.88	17.51	70.9
Kentucky	62.40	6.22	41.10	27.52	56.00	4.90	38.28	22.62	121.7
Louisiana	64.80	7.38	51.61	20.57	60.40	8.34	50.92	17.82	115.4
Mississippi	48.30	7.31	39.08	16.53	61.60	9.19	53.83	16.96	97.5
North Carolina	93.40	5.64	62.15	36.89	114.40	5.82	87.06	33.16	111.2
South Carolina	69.70	7.21	47.93	28.98	56.70	5.68	47.26	15.12	191.7
Tennessee	41.80	7.42	32.70	16.52	52.60	5.52	40.79	17.33	95.3
Texas	30.60	4.47	25.57	9.50	34.10	4.27	31.48	6.89	137.9
Virginia	54.20	2.28	30.84	25.64	58.20	2.34	46.23	14.31	179.2
West Virginia	44.10	—	29.54	14.56	39.10	—	31.31	7.79	186.9

the order of one billion dollars. Second, this important equity base is disappearing at an amazingly rapid rate. In other words, at the very period in which American national policy has begun to focus on the need for fostering minority enterprise, the most important minority equity base is disappearing. Finally, this depletion of minority-owned land resources is all the more paradoxical in view of the evidence that this land is capable of leveraging substantial capital, and of supporting relatively efficient economic enterprises. Given the important changes that are occurring in the economy of the South, the value of this land is likely to increase over time. Accordingly, the economic opportunities for the owners of this land are likely to expand. The great challenge, therefore, is to survive the intervening period during which the pressures for further sales will continue to outweigh the opportunities for economic returns.

EXPANDED OWNERSHIP AS A MINORITY ENTERPRISE STRATEGY: LESSONS FROM THE NEW DEAL'S LAND-REFORM EXPERIMENTS

Before accepting these conclusions, however, it is necessary to look beyond the aggregate data on black landowners and bring the analysis down to a more individualized level. To do this, a sample of black landowners was selected for more detailed scrutiny. The sample consisted of those landowners who received land under an innovative New Deal land-reform experiment called the Resettlement Program.

Launched in 1934 under the auspices of the division of Subsistence Homesteads of the Department of the Interior, and then picked up in succession by the Federal Emergency Relief Administration, the Resettlement Administration, and the Farm Security Administration, the Resettlement Program was designed to relocate southern farm families from worn-out lands onto better farmlands that for one reason or another were not in production. Typically, the federal government would purchase large southern plantations that were in default, break them into smaller farm operations, and sell them to small farmers or tenants on long-term, low-interest loans. Project settlers were required to sign lease-purchase agreements providing an option to buy the unit after a five-year trial rental period. The general plan was to offer successful participants forty-year mortgages at 3 percent interest when the trial

period ended. In the meantime, the Resettlement Administration collected rent on the land and RA local officials worked with the participants in developing detailed farm and home plans. These plans outlined
what crops were to be planted, the number and type of livestock to be
raised, the acreage to be cultivated, and so on. Demonstration agents or
home economists worked with the project women, teaching canning and
food processing. In addition, the government constructed community
buildings, schools, and cooperative enterprises such as cotton gins,
stores, and grist mills at each project; provided for medical assistance
through special arrangements with local physicians; and helped organize
various activities designed to instill a sense of community.[3]

Altogether, 141 agricultural resettlement projects were undertaken
between 1934 and 1943. Of these, 13 were reserved exclusively for
blacks, and an additional 19 so-called scattered farm projects involved
substantial numbers of blacks as well, thus redeeming, albeit on a
meager scale, the Reconstruction dream of "forty acres and a mule" by
distributing approximately 170,000 acres of land on quite favorable
terms to about 2,300 black tenant families.[4]

From the point of view of examining the impact of land on poor
families, the resettlement project thus affords an unusual and unique
opportunity. First, all the recipients of land under this program received
it at about the same time, thus simplifying the problems of making
comparisons among different landowners. Second, the blacks who received land under the resettlement project typically received decent
plantation land, rather than the less fertile hilly land to which blacks
have traditionally been confined in the South. The experiences of these
black landowners thus provide an especially good test of the prospects
for a land-based minority enterprise strategy. Finally, both blacks and
whites received land at about the same time under this program, making
it possible to draw comparisons across racial lines and to gauge the
impact of racial discrimination on black landowners.

The experiences of blacks who received land under the Resettlement
Program thus provided an unusually good—if hardly perfect—test of
the prospects for a land-based minority enterprise strategy. Of special
interest in this regard are the answers to four sets of questions:

   1. How successful are black landowners in holding onto land when
      the land in question is relatively fertile land? Have the blacks who
      received land under the Resettlement Program managed to hold

onto it more successfully than black landowners generally?

2. What is the impact of land on the general well-being of these landowners? Does it improve their income? Their health? Their children's life chances?

3. What is the impact of landownership on civic participation? Do landowners participate more actively in social affairs in their community than do nonlandowners? Do they participate more in political affairs?

4. What is the impact of landownership on the sense of efficacy and the future orientation of these individuals? Do landowners have a greater sense of effectiveness than do nonlandowners?

To answer these questions, eight all-black resettlement projects in five southern states were selected for detailed examination. For each of these projects, detailed title searches were undertaken to determine how long the original recipients of land managed to hold onto it, what success they have had in generating capital against the security of their land, and whether blacks still own the land. In addition, the mortgage experience of that land which has changed from black to white ownership in the intervening thirty years was examined. Finally, all the original recipients of land who could still be located as well as a sample of black tenant farmers in the same counties in which these projects were located were interviewed. The use of a tenant farmer sample was designed to provide a control group against which to compare the landowners. Since the resettlement project participants had themselves been tenant farmers prior to getting the land, the use of a tenant control group made it possible to assess the exact impact that landownership *per se* had on these individuals. Altogether, 178 original project participants and 100 tenant farmers were interviewed, using an extensive twenty-one-page interview schedule and a team of interviewers trained at Duke University's black oral history project.

The results of this work are quite striking, and can be discussed most conveniently under three basic headings: (1) land retention, (2) general well-being, and (3) civic participation.

LAND RETENTION

In a real sense, the most basic test of the Resettlement Program so far as its black participants are concerned is the extent of its success in creating a more or less permanent cadre of black landowners. As the interviews confirmed, all but a handful of the blacks who participated in the program were truly chronic tenants, with no previous contact with landownership.[5] The overwhelming majority, moreover, stressed their eagerness to acquire land and a home in explaining why they took part in the program. "I wanted a home and some land, but people didn't sell land to colored people in here," one Gee's Bend, Alabama, project settler said. "This thing let me have a piece of the world, and it's worth more than money." "There is no getting around the issue," a Mileston, Mississippi, participant concurred. "Land is the single most important thing a man can get for himself and his family."

By installing black tenants on 60- to 100-acre plots of farmland in the early 1940s, however, the Resettlement Program was running headlong against some long-term trends in southern agriculture that were severely undermining the position of the small farmer in general, and the black small farmer in particular. As was pointed out, between 1945 and 1969 the number of black farmowners in the five states of Alabama, Arkansas, Louisiana, Mississippi, and North Carolina, where the sample projects are located, declined from about 74,000 to 30,000, a drop of 59 percent; the amount of black-owned farmland decreased from 4.6 million acres to 2.1 million, a drop of 55 percent.

In view of these trends, how did the resettlement project participants fare? Did the superior land, generally larger plots, and technical assistance made available to black tenants who became owners under the resettlement experiment allow these former tenants to hold their own in the face of these trends? The detailed title searches conducted at the eight resettlement project sites visited make it possible to answer these questions. What they suggest is that 282 of the 556 black families that secured land in these eight projects still held the land—in whole or in part—thirty years later. Altogether, about 17,000 of the 41,000 acres of project land still remained in the hands of the original black participants after thirty years.

These figures drastically understate the extent of black land retention in these projects, however. This is because many of the original participants have since retired or died, leaving their land to other blacks. The real test of retention, therefore, is to ask how many of the original acres deeded to blacks by the federal government still remain in black hands today, whether in the hands of the original owners or other blacks who acquired it. As table 10.8 shows, while the total number of black

TABLE 10.8   Changes in Black Landownership in 8 Former Resettlement Projects and in States Where They Are Located

	Number			Acres		
	1945/1943	1969/1974	% Change	1945/1943	1969/1974	% Change
All black landowners in Ala., Ark., La., Miss., N.C.	73,880	30,002	−59.4	4,584,829	2,073,897	−54.6
Black landowners on land encompassed in 8 former black resettlement projects	556	573	+ 3.1	41,247	29,968	−27.3

Note: The 1945 and 1969 dates are from the Agricultural censuses and apply to the figures for all landowners. The 1943 and 1974 dates apply to the FSA landowners—1943 being the year most titles were transferred and 1974 being the year when title searches were conducted.

landowners in the states where the eight projects were located declined by 59 percent between 1945 and 1969, the number of blacks who owned resettlement project land actually increased by 3.1 percent, even after adjusting for divisions among heirs. Similarly, while the total black-owned acreage in these states declined by 55 percent, the total black-owned acreage on former project lands declined by a substantially smaller 27 percent—about half as much.

The resettlement experiment thus seems to have succeeded moderately well in equipping a group of black tenants with the land and assistance needed to make a go of family farming. More than that, it provided the mechanism for setting aside some relatively good agricultural land for ownership by blacks on a long-term basis, and thus contributed to an absolute increase in the number of black landowners that contrasts sharply with the general decline of these landowners across the South.

WELL-BEING

Although the resettlement experiment thus seems to have been relatively successful in creating a permanent cadre of black landowners, the question still remains whether it was successful in improving the general well-being of these landowners. To answer this question, the sample of landowners, as well as the sample of tenants, was asked a series of questions about their income and assets, as well as about some other indices of well-being. Although the resulting data suggest that the original project participants did not have current incomes substantially larger than those of the tenants in the sample—largely because they are older than the tenants and therefore more likely to be retired—the data do suggest that the project landowners are far ahead of the tenants on a variety of other measures of well-being. For example, the project landowners have been considerably more successful than the tenants in acquiring the critical accouterments of a modest, middle-class life style, at least by rural standards—a car, a refrigerator, an automatic washing machine, a television set, and so on (see table 10.9). Beyond this, of course, the project landowners also owned their homes, which, as one respondent explained, is "the beautifulest thing a man can ever have, to say I'm going home to my own place."

When one looks beyond these physical and monetary manifestations of well-being at the emotional and psychological benefits, even more per-

TABLE 10.9 **Ownership of Various Assets by FSA Participants and Black Tenants**

| | Percent of Total Who Own Recorded Asset | |
	FSA Participants *n = 178*	*Tenants* *n = 93*
Tractor	46.1	29.0
Truck	40.3	32.3
Car	70.2	59.1
Refrigerator	97.2	93.5
Washing Machine	82.0	53.8
Telephone	88.8	53.8
T.V.	96.6	82.8
Cattle (5 head or more)	21.1	8.6

suasive evidence of the long-run impact of the resettlement experience on participant well-being is apparent. For example, data generated by the Health Research Project in Holmes County, Mississippi, indicate that the resettlement project participants in that county are in better nutritional health and have lower levels of hypertension than blacks generally in the county, particularly those owning no land. Interview data seems to confirm this. Tenant interview responses reflect a significantly greater sense of pessimism and timidity than is apparent in FSA-participant responses. For example, 49 percent of the tenants registered agreement with the statement, "These days, a person can't really trust anyone but himself," as compared to only 31 percent of the FSA landowners. By the same token, despite the prevailing norms favoring political participation, close to a third of the tenants expressed disinterest in participation and a sense of complete powerlessness, as compared to only 12 percent of the FSA landowners. Finally, when asked if people ever come to them for help with their problems, half the landowners, but only 30 percent of the tenants, answered yes. Evidently, access to land provided a potent social and pyschological boost to project participants. Their response to an open-ended question inquiring what difference owning land made in their lives speak eloquently and forcefully to this point:

"It has made me feel like a man. I feel like I'm somebody."

"Well, it's made me self-reliant. It put me in a position not to look to other people to look out for me."

"It has made me feel secure. I didn't have to depend on anybody for the things I needed. It has made me feel like a real person."

"It has made me feel more independent than I ever felt in my life."

"Owning land has helped us to live the way we wanted. We worked hard and produced good crops and it was all ours."

"It has been the most important thing in our lives. It has given me a chance to be free."

"It's been a great help. It gives you more recognition if you're a landholder. It gives you more voice."

"Well, it kinda gives you a feeling of security. Helps you hold your head up more and increases your buying power and things like that."

"It made me my own boss. It gave me a home and the security of owning a home. It made me more willing to speak out and stand up."

"It has made quite a bit of difference. It made me more substantial and independent; it has given me bargaining power. Anything I want to do I do not have much trouble because I have a leverage."

"Owning land meant I didn't have to be a slave for somebody else. I always felt independent owning my own land."

The profound sense of heightened self-worth, social standing, and prestige reflected in these comments was apparently not just imagined by the FSA project participants. It found more tangible manifestation as well, most notably in the success with which these former down-and-out tenants established ongoing business relationships with local white enterprises. Data on the loan histories of the project landowners provide perhaps the clearest demonstrations of this point. As part of the land search work, data were collected on all mortgages secured by project land between 1943 and 1973, whether the land remained in black hands or was sold to whites. There is thus available a complete record of the capital-generating capacity of this land, both during the time it was held by blacks and the time it was held by whites.

TABLE 10.10 **Capital Generated by Blacks and Whites through Mortgages on FSA Project Lands,**[a] **1943–1973 (all figures in 1967 dollars)**

	Amount Borrowed				Amount Borrowed per Acre-Year[b]			
	Short-Term	Long-Term	Total	Acre-Years	Short-Term	Long-Term	Total	
Blacks	$3,273,126	$7,324,308	$10,597,433	722,096	$4.53	$10.14	$14.68	
Whites	1,535,320	1,841,261	3,376,581	197,930	7.76	9.30	17.06	

[a]Projects covered were Lakeview, Mileston, Mounds, Tennessee Farm Tenant Security, Tillery, and Townes.
[b]An "acre-year" is one acre of land owned for one year. A landowner who controls a 40-acre plot for ten years thus accounts for 400 acre-years of ownership (40 × 10).

Given what we know about the character of southern rural society during this period, we would expect that blacks would do considerably worse than whites in securing loans, even on the same land. As reported in table 10.10, however, this turns out not to be the case for the FSA landowners. Once all loans have been converted into constant dollars to take account of changes in purchasing power, and adjusted for the length of time and quantity of land accounted for by whites and blacks, the capital-generating ability of the black landowners turns out to be roughly comparable to that of whites.[6] In the case of long-term credit, in fact, the black landowners were actually more successful in generating capital against the security of project land than were white landowners on this same land. Thus black landowners managed to generate an impressive $10.6 million of capital against the security of their project land during the years they were in control of it—an average of $14.68 per acre per year—of which $10.14 per acre per year, or $7.3 million, was long-term credit. The comparable figures for whites were $3.4 million of credit overall, or $17.06 per acre per year, of which $9.30 per acre per year, or $1.8 million, was long-term credit.

To be sure, a considerable portion of the black credit, especially the long-term credit, was provided in the form of the original government loan. However, the white loan figures are probably comparably affected by the fact that loans were frequently taken out against more than one parcel of property—much of it outside the project—yet there was usually no way to determine what portion of the loan to apportion to the project land and what portion to apportion to the nonproject land. Since table 10.10 generally "charges" the full amount of such loans to the project land, it probably overstates the amount of capital raised by white landowners against the security of project land. In view of this, the similarity in the white and black loan figures is all the more striking.

This important finding about the relative success of FSA landowners in generating capital is further supported, moreover, by the landowners' own accounts. Although 79 percent of the project landowners indicated they thought whites had an easier time getting loans or got better terms, and although substantial numbers reported intimidation attempts by white creditors dissatisfied with the landowners' political activity or other behavior, the vast majority (77.7 percent) nevertheless reported "almost no trouble" in getting loans. Of all the types of loans, only land purchase loans seem to have caused any serious problems, and even here the FSA landowners encountered far fewer problems than the tenants.

This is not to say, of course, that ownership of land obliterated all racial discrimination in access to rural credit. Far from it. Loans were still largely tied to farming endeavors and frequently carried stiffer terms than were available to whites. What is more, they were available only in small amounts at a time. Yet there is impressive evidence here to substantiate the view that access to land placed these FSA participants on a far more equal footing than would otherwise have existed, and that it consequently enabled them to establish workable business relationships with local white enterprises and credit sources in ways that contributed significantly to a sense of pride and independence. In short, this mortgage data and reported loan activity seem to lend further support to the notion that the resettlement program made a significant contribution to participant well-being, especially its social and psychological dimensions.

In addition to this data on the well-being of project participants themselves, there is some evidence in the data that these manifestations of well-being carried over to the project participants' children, permitting them to adjust more successfully than the tenants' children to the tensions and problems of migration. Of the 597 FSA participants' children over eighteen years old and in the labor force, for example, 42 percent are in white-collar occupations. By contrast, only 25 percent of the comparable group of tenant children hold such jobs (see table 10.11). Whether this is because of material benefits, more subtle psychological and social impulses, or just happenstance is impossible to determine for certain. However, recent anthropological research demonstrating the vital role that land has played as an anchoring mechanism for the black extended family and underlining the role that this institution has in turn played as a crucial socializing and facilitating mechanism in the black migration process[7] certainly lends credence to the view that the FSA experiments can claim some of the credit for the apparently successful adjustment achieved by the children of the participants.

Though perhaps not fully conclusive, there is substantial evidence here to support the hypothesis that the resettlement experiment made a significant, positive contribution to the well-being of its black participants. Because the amount of land provided to participants under the program was still quite meager on any absolute scale, this impact was

TABLE 10.11   **Occupations of Children of FSA Participants and Black Tenants**

Occupation	FSA Participants n = 597*	Black Tenants n = 261*
Professional, technical, managerial	28.6%	17.2%
Other white collar	13.2	7.3
Blue collar, unemployed	58.1	75.5
Total	99.9%	100.0%

*Includes only children 18 years old and over who are in the labor force

understandably limited in purely economic terms, at least as measured by cash income. In fact, the only notable complaint the participants had about the program as they reflected back on it was that, as one of them put it, "we weren't given enough land to succeed." Even in purely economic terms, however, the program did have an important impact, allowing its participants to acquire the paraphernalia of a modest middle-class life style, at least by rural standards. Beyond that, it seems to have contributed quite significantly to participant well-being in psychological and emotional terms, yielding precisely those attributes of self-reliance that program planners hoped for. Whether these people would have fared better had they not taken part in this experiment but instead joined the migrant stream north is, of course, impossible to say. But it can be said that the program permitted a cadre of former black tenants to survive in the South, to develop a strong sense of self-worth and pride, and to elevate themselves to a modest middle-class social and economic status. In the process, moreover, it seems to have contributed to the success with which the children of these program participants coped with the difficulties of migration themselves.

CIVIC PARTICIPATION

Even more dramatic evidence of the impact of the resettlement program on the black tenants who participated is shown by their civic participation. In a democratic polity, civic involvement and knowledge about civic affairs are central to what it means to be a "self-reliant individual.'' In fact, even participation in social and religious organizations is important since it can provide an antidote to anomie and insecurity and thus help sustain the social fabric and contribute to personal equilibrium.

Because the agricultural depression that began in the 1920s did such damage to rural social institutions, the resettlement program made the fostering of civic participation a central part of its mission. The mere elevation of tenants to owner status, it was felt, would contribute much to this effort, but this was supplemented as well by community organization and citizenship-training activity.

Needless to say, this aspect of the resettlement program was of special importance to rural blacks, whose organizational life and civic involvement had historically been rigidly constrained by the operation of the two-caste system. What is more, as has been noted, access to land could be an especially potent stimulant to civic involvement for blacks since it promised a degree of economic independence, and hence partial release from the debilitating dependency and enforced passivity that constrained black civic participation under the sharecrop system.

Interestingly, the program participants interviewed seemed to think that the resettlement program worked just as this line of reasoning suggests. Asked what difference landownership made in their lives, 84 percent mentioned the sense of independence and security it provided, the chance to ''be your own boss.''

But to what extent did these landowners make use of this independence and take part in civic affairs? The evidence from the survey is striking. In the first place, despite the caste code's informal discouragement of even vicarious black participation in civic affairs through formal communications media, the FSA landlords developed regular contact with outside events through these media, and did so far more extensively than the tenants interviewed.

Beyond this vicarious involvement in civic affairs through the formal communications media, the project participants turned out to be far more intimately involved than the tenants in the organizational lives of their communities, playing important leadership roles in local church and fraternal organizations. For example, 59 percent indicated they had been a deacon or officer in their church, compared to 24 percent of the tenants; 68 percent recorded membership in at least one social organization such as the Masons or Elks, as compared to only 32 percent of the tenants; 26 percent reported holding an office in such an organization, versus only 5 percent of the tenants; and 44 percent claimed membership in a farm cooperative, as against only 9 percent of the tenants.

When the civil rights movement came along in the 1950s and 1960s, therefore, the FSA landowners emerged naturally as crucial local contacts and grass-roots leaders. As table 10.12 reveals, the FSA landowners outdistanced the tenants on virtually every indicator of civil rights movement involvement, and the disparity between the two groups was greater the more dangerous the activity. In fact, a full three-fourths of all the tenants conceded that they had not played a very active role in local civil rights activities at all, even though these activities are now surrounded by a halo of romanticism. By contrast, 53 percent of the FSA project landowners indicated they had played a somewhat active or very active part in the movement.

TABLE   10.12   **Extent of Involvement of FSA Project Landowners and Black Tenants in Various Civil Rights Activities Ranked by Degree of "Dangerousness"**

Activity	FSA Project Landowners n = 177	Tenants n = 91
Attended civil rights organization meetings	73.4%	39.6%
Joined a civil rights organization	49.2	19.8
Worked on voter registration	24.9	6.6
Signed a petition protesting actions by local whites	25.4	2.2
Ran for political office	19.2	7.7
Had an outside civil rights worker living in home	12.4	1.1

Not only were the FSA landowners involved in the civil rights efforts more extensively than the tenants, but they were also involved earlier, during the critical period prior to federal government intervention in the voting rights struggle of 1965. It was during this period, after all, that civil rights involvement was most risky and that a cadre of local activists was most desperately needed. From all indications, the FSA landowners comprised an important part of this cadre of early activists in most of the project counties. This is most clearly evident in voter registration figures. At the time of the interviews, 98 percent of the landowners reported they were registered to vote, compared to 73 percent of the tenants. More importantly, close to 60 percent of the FSA landowners reported challenging the restrictions on black voter registration before the passage of the 1965 Voting Rights Act, compared to only 18.5 percent of the tenants (see table 10.13). Even after discounting these figures somewhat for the age difference between the two groups, this disparity is still striking.

TABLE   10.13   **Timing of First Attempt to Register to Vote by Black FSA Project Landowners and Black Tenants**

Date	FSA Project Participants n = *160**	Tenants *n = 92*
Pre-1965	59.4%	18.5%
1965–present	38.7	54.3
Never	1.9	27.2
	100.0%	100.0%

*Excludes 15 respondents who registered but did not indicate year.

Finally, to complete the picture, this disparity in registration finds reflection in actual voting as well. Ninety-four percent of the FSA landowners claim to have voted in the 1972 presidential election, 89 percent in the 1968 presidential election, and 88 percent in the 1971 or 1972 state election. The corresponding figures for the tenants were 68 percent, 56 percent, and 65 percent. This gap is all the more striking, moreover, in view of the political science findings that political participation is generally highest among persons in the age group of our tenant sample and begins to taper off in the age group represented by the FSA landowners.[8]

What emerges from this data, therefore, is rather strong support for the view that the resettlement experiments had a significant "sleeper effect" in creating an important, black landed middle-class independent and confident enough to shoulder the burden of challenging the two-caste system once conditions became ripe. Freed from the dependency of the sharecrop system and invested with the prestige customarily accorded the landowner in rural society, the FSA landowners emerged as central pillars of local black organizational life, limited though it was. When the civil rights movement appeared, moreover, they were available to give it local roots and nurture it through the critical incubation period prior to formal federal involvement. The resettlement program thus seems to have had a substantial impact on the level of civic participation of its beneficiaries. However, this impact, anticipated in the implicit goals of the agency, at least as conceptualized by some of its personnel, was nevertheless dormant throughout much of the early post-program period, emerging only after more than a decade had elapsed.

SUMMARY AND CONCLUSIONS: SOCIAL REFORM ON THE CHEAP

The resettlement program that was vilified and challenged as a wasteful expenditure of the taxpayers' money thus appears, from the perspective of thirty years, to have been a quite impressive social action undertaking. To be sure, the resettlement projects provided no overall cure for the problems of agricultural overproduction and thus can hardly be defended as central elements in a national farm policy. But as elements of an enlightened antipoverty policy aimed at alleviating the problems of chronic rural poverty and fostering "self-reliant individuals," they have much to recommend them. At least for the blacks who participated, the resettlement program had a substantial, long-term, positive impact, creating a permanent cadre of black middle-class landowners in possession of decent agricultural land and thus able to escape some of the chronic suffering and debilitating dependence so common to black sharecroppers in the South. Partially insulated from the pressures of economic dependence, these farmowners functioned as strategic links in the spread of democracy in the South during the 1960s and served as well to cushion the strains of migration on their children. The one serious drawback was that by restricting its recipients to 60 to 100-acre plots, the program failed to provide them with the wherewithal to take a very active part in the mammoth technical changes that have swept southern agriculture in the past two decades. Yet, it has left behind a base upon which larger-scale, black, land-based enterprises could be built.

Even if the savings to the public in terms of foregone welfare costs are ignored, the benefits of this experiment seem substantial. But what of the costs? What was the price of putting this cadre of black tenants on the road to self-regeneration? Table 10.14 presents the data that are available, showing the net cost to the government for six of the eight projects examined in detail here. The figures are striking. After adding the costs of land purchase, land development, community facilities, and operating expenses, and subtracting the income the government received during the trial rental periods and the returns from sales of project lands, the total outlay for these six projects comes to $1,177,320, or a mere $2,273 per family. If only the costs directly related to the development of the farming units are considered (that is, the costs of the community facilities, many of which were later deeded to local governments, are excluded), the total net cost comes to only $238,041, or $460 per family. Here, certainly, is social reform on the cheap. Even if the "opportunity cost" to government of having its capital tied up in long-term loans to small black farmowners is added, this general conclusion would not change substantially. Considering its long-term impacts, the resettlement experiment—at least as it applied to the blacks in the projects we have examined—seems to have been well worth the cost.

The lessons for policymakers and students of social welfare policy should be clear. In the first place, this evaluation of the resettlement program underlines the importance of a sufficiently long time dimension in evaluating social action undertakings. Evaluators who concentrate exclusively on immediate program impacts and ignore the important "sleeper effects" likely to accompany such policy initiatives are doomed to produce misleading results at best and systematically biased ones at worst. In the process, some of the potentially most promising social action efforts can be erroneously dismissed as ineffective duds and hence scuttled before their true impact can become apparent.[9]

Beyond this, moreover, the resettlement experience provides a powerful demonstration of the value of the "expanded ownership" ap-

TABLE 10.14   Net Cost to Government of 6 All-Black Resettlement Projects as of June 30, 1945*

Project	1 Units Covered	2 Cost of Land + Development (including community facilities)	3 Operating Expenses	4 Income	5 Return on Sales	6 Net Cost (2 + 3)− (4 + 5)	7 Net Cost per Family (6 ÷ 1)	8 Net Cost (−) or Profit (+) per Family (excluding community facilities)
Gee's Bend (Ala.)	88	$ 379,500	$ 71,016	$ 48,860	$ 123,800	$ 277,856	$3,157	−$ 845
Lakeview (Ark.)	124	819,871	141,545	118,058	485,073	358,285	2,889	− 1,074
Mileston (Miss.)	107	730,511	103,375	55,458	592,428	186,000	1,738	− 195
Mounds (La.)	142	768,340	63,739	68,157	548,745	215,177	1,515	+ 24
Prairie (Ala.)	26	148,632	34,144	13,659	87,395	81,722	3,143	− 1,532
Townes (Ark.)	31	163,680	28,053	40,562	150,721	450	15	+ 864
Total	518	$3,010,534	$441,512	$344,754	$1,929,972	$1,177,320	$2,273	$ 460

*Data on the Tillery Project was reported together with the data on the adjoining white project, making it impossible to determine costs for Tillery alone. The same was true for the black and white portions of the Tennessee Farm Tenant Security Project. Accordingly, the data here covers only six of the eight projects examined in this report.

Source: House Appropriations Committee, Hearings, 1946, 1404–1409, 1411–1419. (Costs reported here are pro-rated on the basis of the number of units sold as of June 30, 1945. No such pro-rating was done in the original.)

proach to antipoverty and minority development policy. What it suggests is that by providing the poor with the opportunity to acquire equity resources and thus to escape poverty by their own exertions, public initiatives can have a profound, long-term, positive effect; an effect that may be quite a bit more substantial than those apparently produced by the existing welfare and service programs.

To be sure, the resettlement program was not wholly successful in these respects. The amount of land it provided each participant was, after all, rather meager on any absolute scale, confining participants to fairly limited livelihoods and offering little opportunity for substantial subsequent development. To improve on this record, therefore, future "expanded ownership"-type programs must be more substantial, providing resources ample enough for each participant to make a real start. What should recommend the expanded ownership approach to the attention of policymakers, in other words, is not its cheapness, but its potency and effectiveness, its ability to help people cope with poverty without pushing them into dependence, its proven success in fostering "self-reliant individuals" instead of welfare serfs. These, at any rate, are the lessons of the resettlement program. In an age of widespread cynicism about governmental performance, particularly in the area of social policy, the resettlement program thus provides a refreshing counterexample, and one that may point the way toward a better approach for the future.

PUBLIC LAND AND MINORITY ENTERPRISE

Against the backdrop of an examination of the location, uses, and changes of minority land resources, and the demonstration of the actual impact that land has on the minority poor, it is time to begin considering practical ways to implement a minority business development strategy utilizing existing minority-owned land as a base. To do so, this section examines just one of several possible policy options: the idea of utilizing publicly owned land in conjunction with minority-owned land.

The rationale for this approach derives from the fact that black-owned farms are quite small in size. As a result, per-farm profits are too small to generate an adequate aggregate income. Only if the current minority landowners can gain access to additional land, therefore, can they hope to maintain control of their land as viable agricultural enterprises. How-

ever, outright purchase is exceedingly difficult because of the recent
escalation of land prices, the historic disadvantage blacks have had in
securing credit for land purchase, and the increased cost of rental land.

The utilization of federally owned land by minority landowners offers
a potential solution to this dilemma. As of 1974, the United States
government owned 14.4 million acres of land in Alabama, Arkansas,
Georgia, Louisiana, Mississippi, North Carolina, South Carolina, and
Virginia—12.8 million of it in the hands of civilian agencies. Much of
this federal land is located, moreover, in counties with considerable
black landownership. Of the 293 counties with federal land in these
eight states, 177 also contain 500 or more acres of black-owned land.
Most importantly, much of this federally owned land is now put to
commercial use of one sort or another. If minority landowners could
gain access to this commercially used federally owned land, they could
conceivably gain the critical margin they need to convert their farms
into profitable agricultural enterprises.

To assess the viability of such a strategy, the location and extent of
federal land resources in the South, the relationship between the location of federally owned land and minority-owned land, and the poten-
tials for giving minority landowners access to this federally owned land
were examined in detail. Attention focused particulary on the four federal civilian agencies that own the majority of federal land in the South.
As shown in table 10.15 , these four agencies are the Forest Service of
the United States Department of Agriculture, the Corps of Engineers,
the Fish and Wildlife Service, and the Park Service.

Of the 14.4 million acres of federally owned land in the eight states
investigated, those held by the Forest Service turned out to hold the
greatest promise for use in a minority development strategy. The Forest
Service alone accounts for 9 million of the 14.4 million federally owned
acres of land in these states. As table 10.16 notes, the Forest Service's
holdings stretch across 177 different counties, 86 of which also contain
500 acres or more of black-owned land.

What makes this overlap particularly significant is the pattern of
usage of this forest land. Unlike the national forests of the western
public land states, which were carved out of existing federal landholdings, the southern forests were specifically purchased by the government over the past sixty years largely for conservation purposes, under
the authority of the Weeks Forest Purchase Act of 1911 and subsequent

TABLE 10.15   **Federally Owned Land in 8 Southern States by Agency and State as of June 30, 1971**
(in thousand of acres)

Agency	Ala.	Ark.	Ga.	La.	Miss.	N.C.	S.C.	Va.	Total
Forest Services	634.0	2,454.1	837.2	594.8	1,136.1	1,133.4	594.6	1,531.3	8,915.2
Corps of Engineers	62.6	488.2	323.1	62.1	295.4	58.0	99.9	113.8	1,503.2
Fish & Wildlife	9.0	124.4	428.4	230.9	58.6	113.3	138.1	17.8	1,120.5
Park Service	6.2	5.6	15.4	—	20.9	334.2	4.0	267.5	662.9
Army	170.4	86.1	524.88	116.4	4.5	143.0	53.7	159.3	1,258.1
Navy	3.6	—	10.7	5.0	11.2	116.5	33.5	109.4	289.8
Air Force	5.7	9.4	11.6	25.0	6.2	3.3	14.7	7.1	90.0
TVA	211.6	—	9.5	—	9.2	22.0	—	—	252.3
NASA	—	—	—	—	20.9	—	—	—	20.9
AEC	—	—	—	—	—	—	198.3	—	198.3
Other	4.9	7.0	27.4	4.4	3.9	18.4	14.7	42.4	106.1
Total	1,108.0	3,174.7	2,188.1	1,038.5	1,575.9	1,942.2	1,141.5	2,248.5	14,417.4

Source: Public Land Statistics 1972 (Bureau of Land Management, Washington, D.C.).

TABLE 10.16 **Extent of Black-Owned Land in the Vicinity of U.S. Forest Service (FS) Land in 8 Southern States**

State	All Counties with F.S. Land	F.S. Counties with 500+ Acres of Black Land	Acres of Black Land in F.S. Counties	No. of Black Landowners in F.S. Counties
Alabama	15	12	110,997	1,525
Arkansas	29	5	85,518	795
Georgia	25	10	34,331	264
Louisiana	7	5	38,279	359
Mississippi	33	31	410,434	4,430
North Carolina	25	4	16,498	310
South Carolina	13	13	79,172	1,136
Virginia	30	6	17,284	124
Total	177	86	792,513	8,943

legislation. While this has made the Forest Service particularly attentive
to conservation practices in the southeastern national forests, it has
hardly closed these areas to commercial activity. The southeastern
forests, like those elsewhere in the nation, are managed under the "multiple use and sustained yield" principle incorporated in the Multiple Use
Act of 1960 (15 U.S.C. 528-531). The "multiple use" portion requires
that forest lands be made available for a host of commercial and non-
commercial purposes, including logging, grazing for livestock, wildlife
refuges, hunting, and recreation. The "sustained yield" part of the
standard requires that these uses be regulated in such a way as to:

> . . . achieve and maintain in perpetuity . . . a high-level annual
> or regular periodic output of the various renewable resources of
> the national forests without impairment of the productivity of the
> land. (P.L. 83-517)

As table 10.17 indicates, the national forests in these eight southern
states do generate significant revenues. For the 1973 fiscal year, these
revenues amounted to $24,069,921, about half of it from the forests in
just two states—Mississippi and Louisiana.

TABLE 10.17 **Revenues from National Forests in 8 Southern
States, Fiscal Year 1973**

State	Total Receipts	County Allocation
Alabama	$1,189,454	$ 297,263
Arkansas	4,446,062	968,198
Georgia	1,422,506	355,626
Louisiana	5,742,846	1,435,711
Mississippi	6,649,815	1,662,454
North Carolina	1,010,605	252,693
South Carolina	3,170,446	792,611
Virginia	438,187	101,835
Total	$24,069,921	$5,866,391

For the most part, these revenues derive from a single source: the sale
of timber. In fact, timber operations accounted for more than 90 percent
of all Forest Service collections in the southeastern forests. Moreover,

the greatest volume of timber cutting takes place in the fast-growing loblolly pine forests of Mississippi, Louisiana, and Arkansas, areas which coincidentally have substantial concentrations of black populations and considerable black landownership. From all indications, however, few—if any—blacks take part in this activity except as employees of white-owned firms. In substantial measure, this is a product of the heavy capital investment requirements of logging operations and the frequently risky character of the business. In part, however, it is also the product of lack of information[10] and the character of contracting procedures. Timber rights in the national forests are secured by competitive bidding. Forest Service teams are required to survey and appraise the area to be logged, advertise the sale for thirty days, receive bids, and then award the rights to the highest bidder. In the normal course of events, however, a handful of larger operators can dominate the bidding in each locale. Though Congress attempted to guard against this by enacting a special program setting aside a portion of all timber sales within each forest for small businessmen, most of these allocations are never claimed due to an absence of viable bids.

If timber production is the most significant existing commercial use of the southeastern national forests, grazing is the most significant potential use. Under Forest Service regulations, the Chief of the Service is authorized to permit and regulate the grazing of all kinds of livestock on all National Forest System lands (Code of Federal Regulations 231.1). These lands are made available for livestock use via a permit system under which regional foresters specify, for each rancher using the range, the number of livestock, the grazing period, the grazing system, and the land improvements required.

In 1973 alone, about 17,000 ranchers and farmers purchased permits to graze about 3.2 million cattle and sheep on 105 million acres of forest range land in the national forests and national grasslands in the forty-eight states of the continental United States. Altogether, the national forest accounted for 11 million animal unit months (AUMs) of forage consumption, about 5 percent of all livestock forage consumption in the nation.[11]

Despite a massive increase in cattle production in the southern states over the past decade and a half, grazing in the southeastern national forests has historically been extremely limited. Until 1964, in fact, no permits were issued for grazing in Forest Service lands in the Southeast, and what grazing occurred was done in trespass. Permits have been available since 1964, but only on a temporary, one-year-at-a-time basis that gives ranchers little security over the long term. Although these permits have been relatively inexpensive—10 cents to 25 cents per animal unit month compared to 60 cents to 70 cents on national forest lands elsewhere in the country—they have also been quite limited. As of 1972, for example, fewer than 30,000 livestock, accounting for less than 168,000 animal unit months of forage, were permitted to graze in the forests in the eight states under consideration here. According to one estimate, only about 1,500 grazing permits are outstanding in these states, and no more than 50 of these have been granted to blacks.[12]

The southeastern national forests have far greater grazing potential than these figures might suggest, however. Of the 4,611,855 acres in the National Forest System in the entire South, for example, only 349,695 have been declared off limits for grazing.[13] More directly, the Forest Service's own *Grazing Statistical Report* estimates conservatively that the national forests in these eight states could easily provide more than three times as many animal unit months of forage as are now allowed each year without impairing the land or interfering with other range uses, such as watershed protection and recreation.[14]

From all indications, moreover, the Department of Agriculture is eager to put this excess capacity to use. In December 1973, the department established a special Inter-Agency Work Group on Range Production to explore ways to increase meat production from the nation's ranges, including those under public control.[15] Because of their low utilization for grazing in the past, the lands of the southeastern forests have become a special object for attention. In 1972, in fact, the southeastern regional office of the Forest Service commissioned a major study of grazing possibilities in the southeastern forests. Completed in February 1975, this study contains a wealth of data about actual and potential Forest Service grazing permittees, and demonstrates clearly both the potential for expanded grazing on the southeastern forest lands and the nature of needed Forest Service information and range improvement efforts.[16]

What makes all of this of immense significance to minority enterprise development is the fact that much of the national forest land most suited to expanded grazing is located in the vicinity of substantial black land holdings. The Forest Service has identified six forests in particular as

candidates for expanded grazing activity: the Conecuh in Alabama, the
Kisatchie in Louisiana, the Bienville and DeSoto in Mississippi, and the
Ozark and Oachita in Arkansas. All but two of these are located in
counties that contain sizable black populations and numerous acres of
black-owned land. Altogether, more than 100,000 acres of black-owned
land are situated in the counties that define the perimeters of these
forests (see table 10.18). Under the proper circumstances, access to
national forest grazing land could permit a substantial number of these
farmers to develop profitable beef cattle enterprises.

In addition to the commerical opportunities available to minority
landowners on Forest Service land in the South, additional opportunities
are available from utilization of the land owned by the Corps of Engineers, and to a lesser extent by the Fish and Wildlife Service and the
National Park Service. In each of these cases, extensive commercial use
is already made of the publicly owned land, and this land is located in
close proximity to minority landowners.

While the idea of increasing the access of minority landowners to
publicly owned lands is by no means the only policy option that might
be pursued to aid these landowners, it is certainly one of the least

TABLE   10.18 **Black Landownership and Population in the Vicinity of
National Forest Lands Scheduled for Increased Grazing**

State	National Forest	Unused Grazing Capacity[a] (AUMs)	Acres in NW[b] Full Owner Farms	NW Population
Alabama	Conecuh	24,704	2,328	15,595
Louisiana	Kisatchie	67,931	23,106	80,617
	Bienville			
Mississippi	DeSoto	96,891	79,631	105,642
	Ozark			
Arkansas	Oachita	157,849	31,249	60,578
	St. Francis			
Total		347,375	136,314	262,432

[a]These are conservative estimates based on the Forest Service's 1972 *Grazing
Statistical Report.*
[b]NW=Nonwhite

expensive. At very little cost to the public in the form of technical assistance and related loan capital, the available existing public land could provide small farmers the critical margin they need to turn their enterprises into profitable operations.

In addition to the opportunities available to minority landowners from the use of publicly owned land, additional opportunities are also available from the spillover effects of major development projects occurring in the vicinity of minority landholdings. With aid from the Office of Minority Business Enterprise, the Duke-OMBE land project has compiled a compendium of major development projects in the South likely to impinge on minority landowners.[17] Equipped with this information, landowners can learn in advance of major developments scheduled for their area, and thus take the actions that are needed to participate in these developments rather than be hurt by them. Needless to say, however, these data will not solve any problems on their own. To be effective, they must be picked up and used by local groups eager to take advantage of the economic opportunities available to minority landowners. For this to occur, however, organized efforts and suitable technical assistance will be required.

CONCLUSION

The past decade and a half of southern history has been one of extraordinary economic growth and development. It is one of the great ironies of this period of history, however, that it has also witnessed the massive decline of probably the most significant equity resource in the hands of minority groups in this nation. For those concerned about the future of minority enterprise, this paradox must be a subject for grave concern because the loss of minority-owned land means the loss of a critical equity base for leveraging capital for a host of economic enterprises. While some of this land is admittedly unproductive and noneconomic, much of it lies right astride the path of southern development, and therefore potentially holds great promise as a development resource. To reverse the prevailing trends and make use of this unique equity resource, however, will require extensive effort—effort to educate owners and their heirs about the development potential of their land, and effort to mobilize governmental resources to provide the needed technical and financial assistance to allow blacks to take advantage of this potential.

Minority-owned land in the American South thus constitutes at once a crisis and an opportunity. The crisis reflects the rapid depletion of this crucial and unique minority equity resource. The opportunity grows out of the possibility of slowing this trend and then utilizing minority-owned land as a foundation for greater minority participation in the dramatic economic development activities occurring in the southern region. Which of these two alternatives prevails, however, will probably be determined in the next decade.

NOTES

1. President's Advisory Council on Minority Business Enterprise, *Minority Enterprise and Expanded Ownership: Blueprint for the 1970s* (Washington, D.C.: U.S. Government Printing Office, 1971), p. 33.

2. Commercial farms are those that sell over $2,500 worth of produce yearly or sell $50-$2,500 yearly if the owner is under 65 and does not work off the farm 100 days or more.

3. Donald Holley, "The Negro in the New Deal Resettlement Program," *New South,* vol. 27, no. 1 (Winter 1972), pp. 58–60; Paul K. Conkin, *Tomorrow a New World: The New Deal Community Program* (Ithaca, N.Y.: Cornell University Press, 1959), pp. 197–209; personal interview with James Bryant, FSA director at Mounds Farm, Talulah, La., February 8, 1974.

4. Because the resettlement project grouped together a host of undertakings launched by several different agencies, these numbers are necessarily rather rough. They are based on material available in the following sources: U.S. Congress, House Committee on Appropriations, *Hearings on the Agriculture Department Appropriation Bill for 1947,* 79th Congress, 2d Sess., p. 1390; Conkin, *Tomorrow a New World,* pp. 199–202; Holley, "The Negro in the New Deal Resettlement Program," pp. 53–65; Sidney Baldwin, *Poverty and Politics: The Rise and Decline of the Farm Security Administration* (Chapel Hill: University of North Carolina Press, 1968), pp. 111–13, 214–17, 336–39; Richard Sterner, *The Negro's Share: A Study of Income, Consumption, Housing and Public Assistance* (New York: Harper and Brothers, 1943), pp. 307–9, 423–24; U.S. Congress, House Committee on Agriculture, *Hearings of the Select Committee to Investigate the Activities of the Farm Security Administration,* 78th Cong., 1st Sess. (1943), part 3, pp. 1124–31.

5. Only 13 of the 178 program participants interviewed indicated they had ever owned land before the resettlement program appeared.

6. Conversion of all loans to constant dollars was necessary because the black landowners tended to own the land during the early period, when the dollar was worth more. Hence their loans would appear artificially small compared to those taken out by whites later, even if they represented the same amount of purchasing power. To correct for this, all loan amounts were converted to 1967 dollars. The adjustment for span and scope of ownership was accomplished by multiplying the number of acres by the number of years of ownership for each owner to give the number of "acre-years" and then adding the number of "acre-years" accounted for by black and white owners separately.

7. Demitri Shimkin, Gloria Louie, and Dennis Frate, *The Black Extended Family: A Basic Rural Institution and a Mechanism of Urban Adaptation,* 9 International Congress of Anthropological and Ethnological Sciences, 1973.

8. See, for example, Lester Milbrath, *Political Participation* (Chicago: Rand-McNally, 1965). For evidence on the drop-off in participation at the upper end of the age scale in the 1972 presidential election, see *U.S. Statistical Abstract* (1973), p. 379.

9. For a fuller discussion of these points, see Lester M. Salamon, "Follow-Ups, Let-Downs, and Sleepers: The Time Dimension in Policy Evaluation," in Charles Jones, ed., *Public Policy Yearbook* (Beverly Hills, Calif.: Sage Publications, 1976).

10. On this point, see Glen Howze, "Forestry and the Black Landowner," paper prepared for the Workshop on the Development Potential of Black-Owned Land, Duke University, December 6, 1974.

11. U.S. Department of Agriculture, *Opportunities to Increase Red Meat Production from Ranges of the USA,* Phase 1 of a report of the USDA Inter-Agency Work Group on Range Production, June 1974, p. 94.

12. Personal interview, Jimmy Wilkens, Range Management Specialist, U.S. Forest Service, Region 8, Atlanta, Ga., August 12, 1974.

13. U.S. Department of Agriculture, Forest Service, *Analysis of Grazing Programs on National Forests in the Southern Region,* report prepared by James E. Morrow, Robert L. Chaffin, and Joseph C. Horvath, February 1975, p. 27.

14. U.S. Department of Agriculture, Forest Service, *Annual Grazing Statistical Report, 1972.*

15. U.S. Department of Agriculture, *Opportunities to Increase Red Meat Production from Ranges of the United States,* Phase 1 of a report of the USDA Inter-Agency Work Group on Range Production, June 1974, pp. 10–11.

16. *Analysis of Grazing Programs on National Forests in the Southern Region.* I am grateful to Carl Holt, Range Management Specialist, U.S. Forest Service, Region 8, for permission to see a prepublication copy of this report.

17. Lester M. Salamon, *Economic Development and Minority Landowners: A Compendium of Major Public and Private Development Projects in Areas of Substantial Minority Landownership in the South,* Washington, D.C.: Office of Minority Business Enterprise, U.S. Department of Commerce, March 1976).

INDEX

About the Contributors

Robert Boone
Director of Public Service
Tennessee State University
Nashville, Tennessee

Joseph Brooks
Executive Director
Emergency Land Fund
Atlanta, Georgia

Dr. James A. Lewis
Economic Statistics and
    Cooperative Services
U.S. Department of Agriculture
Washington, D.C.

Dr. Leo McGee
Assistant Dean
Extended Services
Tennessee Technological University
Cookeville, Tennessee

Dr. Manning Marable
Associate Professor
Department of History
University of San Francisco
San Francisco, California

Dr. Carl H. Marbury
Vice President for Academic
Affairs/Dean
Garrett-Evangelical Thelogical
    Seminary
Evanston, Illinois

Dr. William E. Nelson, Jr.
Chairperson
Department of Black Studies
Ohio State University
Columbus, Ohio

Dr. Charles Nesbitt
Assistant Professor and Director
Community Extension Center
Department of Black Studies
Ohio State University
Columbus, Ohio

Dr. Frank G. Pogue
Chairperson
Department of African/Afro-
    American Studies
State University of New York
Albany, New York

Dr. Lester M. Salamon
Director
Urban and Regional Development
    Policy
Institute of Policy Sciences and
    Public Affairs
Duke University
Durham, North Carolina